The Christmas Countdown

Creating 25 Days of
New Advent Traditions for Families

MARGIE J. HARDING

PARACLETE PRESS
BREWSTER, MASSACHUSETTS

The Christmas Countdown: Creating 25 Days of New Advent Traditions for Families

2010   First Printing
2011   Second Printing

ISBN: 978-1-55725-698-0

Scripture quotations are taken from the HOLY BIBLE, NEW INTERNATIONAL VERSION®. Copyright © 1973, 1978, 1984 by Biblica, Inc.™. Used by permission of Zondervan. All rights reserved.

The map of Israel printed on page 121 is taken from www.giltravel .com. Used by permission. All rights reserved.

Front cover image copyright © Richard Sellmer Verlag, www .advent-calendar.com

All music lyrics are in the public domain.

Library of Congress Cataloging-in-Publication Data
Harding, Margie J.
     The Christmas countdown : creating 25 days of new Advent traditions for families / Margie J. Harding.
        p. cm.
     Includes index.
     ISBN 978-1-55725-698-0
     1. Advent. 2. Families—Religious life. I. Title.
     BV40.H3525 2010
     263'.912--dc22   2010025977

10 9 8 7 6 5 4 3 2

Published by Paraclete Press
Brewster, Massachusetts
www.paracletepress.com
Printed in the United States of America

Contents

Introduction

Christmas makes my heart sing. The joy that emanates from almost everyone I see causes my heart to expand in sheer delight. This feeling of elation that began 2,000 years ago in an ancient world continues to bring wonder to Christians every year. A brilliant star led the shepherds and Wise Men to a humble place—a stable in Bethlehem. These unlikely participants were on their way to give the long-awaited King expensive gifts and honor. Their journey created a practice that continues today.

We give gifts to those we love in the tradition of the Wise Men and worship the King in the manner of both the Wise Men and the lowly shepherds. We search our minds and make ready our hearts to welcome the Messiah anew each Christmas season. In a time in history when the secular world sometimes alienates and robs us of this glorious regeneration and encourages us to focus more and more on ourselves instead of what we really deserve and desire, our Advent journey can be aided by readings and activities that refocus us on Christ and light our path with joy and giving. It is my desire that this *Christmas Countdown* will help create in your household a season of waiting, of wonder, of loving others, and of truly expecting Jesus.

Advent is the season of preparation for our King, Jesus, who came in the form of a humble child. Traditionally it is also a season for anticipating the Second Coming, when Jesus will return in glory to carry his faithful believers to everlasting life.

This book will help you prepare your hearts and homes for his coming. Each day of Advent includes a suggested Scripture reading with a key verse, questions to reflect on, and a fun activity that can be done as a family. Adults have a challenge to consider and children have prompts to help them focus on a specific idea. Many of the days also provide the lyrics to a Christmas carol to sing, a tradition that seems to have begun for the English as early as 1426 when wassailers (people who went from house to house singing) used music put together by John Audelay, who was both a priest and a poet.

The first week's devotions and activities examine ways we get ready for the coming of the Messiah. As you prepare this week, remember it's essential to slow down, tune out all the "noise," and tune in to God. The second week of Advent asks the question, "Who is waiting?" The devotions explore those who waited for the Christ before he was born and those who wait today for his return. Week three asks, "Why are we waiting?" and week four emphasizes Jesus' birth. The Christmastide section offers ideas for Christmas Eve and Christmas Day, and onward into the rest of the season, which comes to an end on Epiphany, January 6.

Each day encourages family members to learn more about themselves and more about this wondrous season through the Scriptures. As you get more involved in Advent, you'll gain understanding and you'll grow. Enjoy this season this year more than ever before and celebrate the greatest birth ever known. Capture the joy that comes with knowing Christ. Delight in his word through this special time, as we center our lives and hearts on his teachings.

ADVENT
Week

1

Getting Ready

Day 1

Busy, but Important?

READ

Malachi 3:1–6

KEY VERSE

"See, I will send my messenger, who will prepare the way before me. Then suddenly the Lord you are seeking will come to his temple; the messenger of the covenant, whom you desire, will come," says the LORD Almighty. (Mal. 3:1)

I have much to do this holiday season. My list of gifts to buy for family and friends gets longer and longer; I try to anticipate who might give our family a gift (so that I don't miss giving them one in return), and so I end up adding the package delivery person, the mail carrier, and the young woman at the bank who is always so helpful, among others. Christmas cards wait to be signed, addressed, stamped, and mailed. I need to begin early to plan a menu for the houseful of family who will be arriving a full week before the holiday. The employees of my husband's business have to be contacted about the celebration planned for them in our home. We've already been invited to two parties that we are expected to attend. My cleaning chores seem overwhelming—I want the house as perfect as possible for our holiday guests. And the pile of gifts to wrap will be enormous. The list goes and on and on. The busyness of the season often leaves me so frayed by Christmas day that I am unable to completely enjoy it. I only want to rest!

I am not the only person who gets caught up in the exhausting cycle we have created for ourselves during the Christmas season. People worldwide become so consumed (and consumer-oriented) that we miss the real meaning of Christmas. Remember, Scripture tells us that a messenger was coming to prepare the way for the Messiah. John the Baptist had that mission. It was he who pleaded with the people to prepare their hearts for Jesus. John wasn't concerned with cooking, cleaning, buying gifts for others, or attending holiday functions. He was concerned about the preparation of hearts to accept the promised King. He was concerned about repentance and making ready the lives of those who have long been awaiting the Christ.

We should be more like John the Baptist. Cleaning, cooking, and parties are irrelevant when compared to preparing our hearts for Jesus. This is the single most important item to remember this holiday season. Jesus is the world's greatest gift. He is the gift to be shared above all others with family and friends. It is not only my responsibility to share this gift, but also my joy.

CONSIDER

1. Which tradition of Christmas is most important to your family and why?
2. Is there anything you do that could be eliminated without losing the "Christmas spirit" to help you feel less overwhelmed?

FAMILY ACTIVITY
Create an Advent wreath

• •

The Advent wreath most likely has its origins in Germany and northern Europe as one of many symbols of light used by Christians in the Middle Ages to celebrate the Christmas season. It may go back to even earlier times. The candles symbolically were placed in a circular evergreen wreath, which represented not only victory and glory, but also the eternity of God and everlasting life. Tradition evolved so that on each Sunday of Advent the candles are lit to proclaim the coming of the Christ Child, the Light of the World. It is customary to say a prayer and sing a hymn with the lighting of the candles. Additionally, some families will extinguish all other lights in the home to allow only the glow of the candles to permeate the room as they reflect on the upcoming joyous celebration.

MATERIALS NEEDED

- four purple candles (or three purple and one pink)
- one white candle
- a Styrofoam holder (or a ring of florist Oasis) for candles or other candleholders
- a base for the wreath (perhaps a plate or a tray)
- greenery to decorate (artificial or fresh). You can use holly, fern, cedar, pine needles and pinecones, or any other evergreens that are available in your area.

Place the four purple candles in a circle in the Styrofoam holder or other candleholders on the base being used. Place the white candle in the center. Arrange the greenery around the bottom of the candles in a way that is pleasing to the eye. On this first Sunday of Advent, light the first purple candle, the "Candle of

Hope," as we celebrate the coming of our King. Reread today's Scripture from Malachi 3:1–6. Sing the carol "It Came Upon the Midnight Clear." (If you don't know the tune, simply read the verses below.) Pray a prayer of hope, thanking God for sending his son, Jesus, who brought the world out of darkness into light. When you have finished, carefully blow out the candle. The remainder of the candles will be lit on consecutive Advent Sundays.

You might want to place a bookmark at this page so that you can easily find the instructions for the next three Sundays of Advent.

On the second Sunday of Advent, light the first candle and a second purple candle, the "Candle of Preparation," as we get ready for the coming of our King. Pray a prayer of preparation, asking God to prepare each heart, mind, and spirit for the coming Savior. And again, thank God for sending Jesus.

On the third Sunday of Advent, light the previous two candles and then light a third candle (pink or another purple), the "Candle of Joy." As we celebrate with joy, pray a prayer of thanksgiving to God, for a love so great to personally draw us to him, to become his children, and to offer eternal life with him in heaven.

On the fourth Sunday of Advent, light all previous candles and the last purple candle, the "Candle of Love." Pray a prayer of love to our gracious God, who loved us so deeply that he anticipated our need and sent his beloved Son to show us the way to be with him forever. On Christmas morning begin your celebration by lighting all previous candles and finally the white candle in the center, as we celebrate the birth of the Messiah. Take time as the day begins to thank God for his unending love, and for his Son, Jesus.

It Came Upon the Midnight Clear

It came upon the midnight clear,
That glorious song of old,
From angels bending near the earth,
To touch their harps of gold;
"Peace on the earth, good will to men,
From heaven's all gracious King."
The world in solemn stillness lay,
To hear the angels sing.

Still through the cloven skies they come
With peaceful wings unfurled,
And still their heavenly music floats
O'er all the weary world;
Above its sad and lowly plains,
They bend on hovering wing,
And ever over its Babel sounds
The blessèd angels sing.

Yet with the woes of sin and strife
The world has suffered long;
Beneath the angel strain have rolled
Two thousand years of wrong;
And man, at war with man, hears not
The love-song which they bring;
Oh hush the noise, ye men of strife
And hear the angels sing.

All ye, beneath life's crushing load,
Whose forms are bending low,
Who toil along the climbing way
With painful steps and slow,
Look now! for glad and golden hours
Come swiftly on the wing.
Oh rest beside the weary road,
And hear the angels sing!

For lo! the days are hastening on,
By prophet-bards foretold,
When with the ever circling years
Comes round the age of gold;
When peace shall over all the earth
Its ancient splendors fling,
And the whole world send back the song
Which now the angels sing.

—EDMUND H. SEARS, 1849

ADULT CHALLENGE

John the Baptist's message was sharing the Good News and repentance. Ask God to place in your heart someone in your workplace or community you could pray for, perhaps someone who is struggling with issues that you don't even know about, or whose faith and hope have become frayed. Pray for this person and record your prayers, thoughts, and feelings on this journey.

CHILD PROMPT

To me, getting ready for Christmas means _____

_____

_____

Day 2

A Reason to Celebrate

READE
READ
Luke 3:1–16

KEY VERSES
John said to the crowds coming out to be baptized by him.... "Do not begin to say to yourselves, 'We have Abraham as our father.' For I tell you that out of these stones God can raise up children for Abraham." (Lk. 3:7–8)

Some of my family traveled the country in an RV for months at a time and told me of the striking differences they experienced while visiting several churches along the way. One of the congregations seemed lifeless to them, with very little enthusiasm and what seemed to be dwindling attendance. In another town they visited a church where they could feel the spirit of God in a very literal sense. They discovered yet another church that was different from the second one, but yet also seemed to be filled with praise and worship. They are already looking forward to returning there.

I wondered if a "lifeless" church might reflect what God's people were like at the time of Jesus' birth, before John the Baptist began preaching in the desert? Many of the people were sorrowful and sad. They felt oppressed by the Romans; they felt distanced from God. Perhaps they couldn't feel God's presence.

Meanwhile, the other two churches may resemble what the people were like when they went to hear John's preaching. John baptized many of these same people. Their hope was rekindled and they heard of the coming of one who was more powerful than he. I imagine those crowds singing, praising God, and rejoicing in their faith and hope.

As we prepare ourselves for this Christmas season, we need to remember there is a reason to celebrate! It has nothing to do with anything ordinary. It is something that happened 2,000 years ago. We were given an incredible gift: the Christ Child who ultimately sacrifices his very life that we may have eternal life with him. It is with this joy that we sing and praise him. It is with this joy that we celebrate!

CONSIDER

1. Why do you and your family attend church? What is your favorite part?

2. In what way could you improve your worship time?

FAMILY ACTIVITY

Secret Santas or
Secret Angels gift exchange

Exchanging gifts at Christmas reminds us of the gifts the Wise Men brought to baby Jesus. Each brought something special: gold, frankincense, and myrrh. They didn't bring gifts with the expectation of getting something in return. They gave the gifts in honor and love of the newborn King.

The Secret Santa/Angel gift exchange furthers this idea with fun and secrecy. Kids love it, and it's a way of involving them in what it truly means to give a thoughtful gift to someone they care for. Decide who will participate in the gift giving. It may be your immediate family or your extended family, or neighbors nearby, or part of your church family. Everyone's name is written on a small piece of paper, which is put into a container and then mixed up. Each participant retrieves a name from the container and keeps it secret. (This may be the hardest part for young children, since in excitement they might want to share who their "secret person" is.)

✵

Decide on a gift (or an act of kindness) for your secret person that you think would bring pleasure and display your affection. It need not be expensive. Wrap the gift, writing only the recipient's name on it. At the designated time, either place all the gifts together, or place yours in a special place that will surprise the recipient—perhaps on their desk, on a favorite chair, in the car, etc. Each person in turn will find his or her gift and then try to guess who the Secret Santa/Angel is. Maybe the Secret Santa/Angel will reveal his or her identity—or choose to keep it a secret forever!

Hark! The Herald Angels Sing

Hark! The herald angels sing,
"Glory to the newborn King!
Peace on earth, and mercy mild,
God and sinners reconciled."
Joyful, all ye nations rise,
Join the triumph of the skies;
With the angelic host proclaim:
"Christ is born in Bethlehem."

Refrain:
Hark! The herald angels sing,
"Glory to the newborn King!"

Christ by highest heav'n adored;
Christ the everlasting Lord!
Late in time behold him come,
Offspring of a Virgin's womb,
Veiled in flesh the Godhead see;
Hail the incarnate Deity,
Pleased as man with man to dwell,
Jesus, our Emmanuel.
[Refrain]

Hail the heav'n-born Prince of Peace!
Hail the Sun of Righteousness!
Light and life to all he brings,
Ris'n with healing in his wings.
Mild he lays his glory by,
Born that man no more may die.
Born to raise the sons of earth,
Born to give them second birth.
[Refrain]

—CHARLES WESLEY, 1739

ADULT CHALLENGE

Reread the Scripture and meditate on Jesus, shutting out all other sounds and listening for his voice. Are you filled with the joy of Jesus' birth? In what new way could you express your joy?

CHILD PROMPT

My favorite part of Christmas is _____

_____

_____

Day 3

Missing the Answer

READ
Psalm 80:1–7

KEY VERSE
Restore us, O God; make your face shine upon us, that we may be saved.
(Ps. 80:3)

We all have dreams. Some are those that come along with age, such as finishing high school, graduating from college, marrying, and having a family. We might dream of owning a home, a new car, or other material things. Other dreams may be more daunting, for instance, a career change after thirty years, becoming a world traveler when it is beyond our present means, or striking it rich!

Dreams often become reality when we apply ourselves prayerfully and steadfastly to that goal. Some dreams, however, can only be attained if God chooses to make certain events happen in our life. Our dreams may seem unrealistic even to us and leave us crying, "Lord, if it's your will, please make it work out!"

About twenty years ago a friend of mine traveled to another part of the country on a family vacation. She and her husband visited an area that stole their hearts. Since that time, they have been praying that circumstances would permit them to move there. They did the necessary research and even requested a job transfer. It didn't happen. So far, they are still waiting. There were times when they nearly gave up the dream: it seemed as though it just wasn't meant to be. Still, the couple visits the favorite area almost yearly and they continue to dream and pray, "Lord, if it's your will, please make the necessary circumstances work out."

The psalmist is praying in the Scripture reading for the people of Israel. He wonders if his prayer is even being heard. Is God angry? Why the delay? Are they asking for the right thing with the right attitude? Are there those who doubt God can save them? Still, the psalmist doesn't doubt that God is there, so he continues to pray on Israel's behalf for God to restore them. They have to wait patiently for God's time. They also have to wait for the *way* God will restore them. They must recognize God's answer.

In his time, God did send an answer. He sent Jesus. Jesus was the Savior for whom they prayed, and yet many missed it. The answer didn't come in the form they expected. The Messiah came as a babe in a manger. He came humbly with a message of peace, hope, and love.

CONSIDER

1. Do you sometimes feel like the psalmist waiting for an answer to a prayer? How does waiting for God's time make you feel?

2. Do you see the world today as the psalmist saw Israel years ago?

FAMILY ACTIVITY
Make your own wrapping paper

Gift wrapping not only hides the gift from the recipient until it is time for opening, but it also tells a little about both the giver and the person receiving the gift. Create your own wrapping paper that shares your creativity and your love.

MATERIALS NEEDED

- white craft paper, butcher paper, or brown paper (from grocery bags)
- scissors
- glue
- stickers
- sparkle sprinkles
- felt-tip markers (water based)
- nontoxic tempera paint
- paintbrushes

- containers for paint
- newspaper
- cookie cutters (for cutouts)
- sponges
- a cut potato
- construction paper
- and other supplies you choose to use for decorations

Place newspaper over your work area for protection against spills. Each person should receive a plain piece of white or brown paper to be decorated. The size can vary according to age and interest.

Using the materials chosen for decorating, create spontaneous designs, holiday scenes, or specific patterns. The cookie cutters can be used for tracing designs on construction paper that are cut and glued onto the paper. The sponges can be cut into shapes, then dipped into the paint and pressed on the paper. The cut potato half can also be made into a stamp. Use stickers, sprinkles, and markers to enhance your artwork. Just have fun! Let the paper dry overnight before wrapping any gifts.

• •

What Child Is This?

What Child is this who, laid to rest,
On Mary's lap is sleeping?
Whom angels greet with anthems sweet,
While shepherds watch are keeping?
This, this is Christ the King,
Whom shepherds guard and angels sing;
Haste, haste, to bring him laud,
The babe, the Son of Mary.

Why lies he in such mean estate,
Where ox and ass are feeding?
Good Christians, fear, for sinners here
The silent Word is pleading.
Nails, spear shall pierce him through,
The cross be borne for me, for you.
Hail, hail the Word made flesh,
The babe, the Son of Mary.

So bring him incense, gold, and myrrh,
Come peasant, king to own him;
The King of kings salvation brings,
Let loving hearts enthrone him.
Raise, raise a song on high,
The Virgin sings her lullaby.
Joy, joy for Christ is born,
The babe, the Son of Mary.

—WILLIAM C. DIX, 1865

ADULT CHALLENGE

Make a bulleted list of your dreams. Consider the possible answers. Consider the possibilities that you might not immediately recognize.

CHILD PROMPT

I dream of the day . . . What do you wish for and why? _____

_____

_____

Day 4

Half Service

Psalm 40

KEY VERSES
Sacrifice and offering you did not desire, but my ears you have pierced; burnt offerings and sin offerings you did not require. Then I said, "Here I am, I have come—it is written about me in the scroll." (Ps. 40:6–7)

We become a society where one half is nearly good for everything! In every grocery store you can find the "lite" version of substances that science says can harm your body. There are "lite" drinks claiming less sugar, crackers claiming less salt, and frozen dinners with half the calories! There are exercise equipment and pills that claim you can lose weight in half the time.

Our days are filled with ways to cut down on time. The appeal is to find the next new thing that will make our life easier so we have more time to enjoy ourselves. Often, however, all these "things" actually make life more complicated. Computers are great until they freeze. Automobiles are indispensable, but they require near-constant maintenance. Elevators save walking, but our society has become obese because of lack of exercise. These "things" require extra time because each creates its own set of issues.

This effort to hurry up our lives often carries over into our spiritual lives as well. A minister friend recently told me that he was reprimanded for preaching "three minutes over" his allotted time. But aren't we cheating ourselves?

We become so wrapped up in other things that we don't have time for God. Our moments are so few that taking the time to read God's word or have conversations with our Maker just doesn't seem to fit in.

God created a wonderful world. He created humans with a mind to invent things, and this is good. But he also sent his Son who gave all. Our sacrifices and burnt offerings and half effort isn't what God desires—he wants all of us. We have reason to exalt in the Lord. It is our responsibility and our joy to spend time with him. We should not be in a hurry and want the "lite" version of his love. We should embrace him with all that we are because Jesus came and gave all that he had.

CONSIDER

1. What does giving only part of ourselves suggest about us to others? What does it suggest about our society?
2. This Advent, what are some ways you could slow down, wait for God, and listen for his word and love for you and your family?

FAMILY ACTIVITY
Create handmade Christmas cards

Making beautifully decorated Christmas cards to share is part of the tradition of Christmas all over the world. As a family create your own Christmas cards for the special people in your lives and share your own unique gifts.

MATERIALS NEEDED

- card stock
- colored or white paper—or you may choose to buy paper that has a Christmas border (found in the craft section)
- envelopes to "match"
- Christmas stamps with ink pads or Christmas stickers
- scissors
- felt-tip markers
- glitter
- glue

Cut the sheet of paper so that folded in half it will fit in your envelope. Decorate the outside of each card with Christmas stamps, stickers, glitter, and markers. Write a special message or note to the receiver of each card on the inside (verses you can use are shown below, or create your own). Decorate the back of the envelope to match the card.

Verse suggestions

- The joy of Christmas is found in the Christ Child;
- To celebrate life . . . To celebrate love . . . Is to celebrate Christmas;
- Christmas . . . Caring with our Heart, Celebrating the Son;
- Ambitions of men pale / Next to the single birth / That brought love to earth;

- What would Christmas be without Jesus? . . . an empty celebration;
- Wishing you Christmas tidings . . . peace, joy, hope and love;
- May you feel the spirit of Christmas all year;
- May Christmas joy empower you to accomplish great things in the coming year.

ADULT CHALLENGE

Assess your relationship with God. Are there areas where you go "lite"? If so, how could you improve them?

CHILD PROMPT

Jesus gave his life for me. I could give a better effort in _____

_____

_____

Day 5

Discipline Teaches

READ

Luke 1:11–23

KEY VERSES

The angel answered, "I am Gabriel. I stand in the presence of God, and I have been sent to speak to you and to tell you this good news. And now you will be silent and not able to speak until the day this happens, because you did not believe my words, which will come true at their proper time." (Lk. 1:19–20)

My husband tells the story of the day he found it necessary to discipline all five of our children for the same misbehavior. He had finally gotten every bedroom repainted in our house. All that was left was to move the furniture back into place. Our youngest son, who was barely two, had somewhere found an ink pen. He deliberately and carefully drew a line all the way around one of the rooms on the freshly painted wall!

A family rule that the children must keep all pens and pencils out of the reach of the youngest clearly had been broken. All were held responsible since no one would take the blame. The punishment wasn't severe but the heartbreak was palpable! Even knowing that the children understood they were responsible, as parents we felt it necessary to impose discipline so they could learn we were serious about consequences when they misbehaved.

Our Scripture tells us of the punishment Zechariah suffered when he doubted the word of God delivered by the messenger Gabriel. It isn't hard to imagine him questioning the possibility of having a child since he and his wife were well past childbearing years. Zechariah didn't mean to doubt God. The angel's words simply didn't seem logical, so he questioned. His doubt, however, cost him his speech for the duration of Elizabeth's pregnancy. God needed to show the people that even the impossible is possible with God.

There are times when we all do and say things we don't mean. We are human and so we fail. God sent his Son so that our failings can be forgiven. It is because of God's grace that we are able to continue daily with hope and promise.

CONSIDER

1. Have you ever heard something directly related to you, your family, or your close friends that you found impossible to believe? How did you react?
2. Was there a time when you thought discipline was unfair? Has your attitude changed?

FAMILY ACTIVITY
Create a gift basket or box

Part of the English Christmas tradition includes Boxing Day, celebrated on December 26. There are varying descriptions of how this tradition began. Most of them include the idea of wealthier people giving gifts of food, clothing, and money to those less fortunate, whether they were servants, workers on a landlord's estate, or tradesmen and clerks. One story claims the tradition began with groups of boys collecting money in boxes from neighbors on the day after Christmas, in honor of the feast day of Saint Stephen, the first Christian martyr. Some families create boxes of treats, small gifts, or coins to be shared with visitors who come calling on the first weekday after Christmas. I like this last idea! You too can create "gift boxes" in the English tradition, but instead of giving them to visitors, give the boxes to brighten the day of people who aren't having a particularly happy Advent season.

MATERIALS NEEDED

- a basket or a box
- tissue paper
- stickers
- crayons/markers
- ribbon
- gifts to fill the box: food items such as canned goods, candy, snacks, baked goods, fruit, and nuts; postage stamps; sticky note pads; books; lotions; gift certificates; and small toys for children

First decide to whom you would like to give a box, and assemble the small gifts. Are there homeless people in your town or city who might welcome a box of food or toiletries? Do you know any elderly neighbors who might enjoy a basket of cookies and cocoa mix? Would patients in a nursing home appreciate a box filled with Christmas cards, pretty pens, and postage stamps?

Decorate the tissue paper with stickers, crayons, or markers. Line the basket or box with decorated tissue paper. Place your chosen items inside. Tie a ribbon around the box or basket handle to add a festive touch. Include a note if you wish.

● ●

O Come, O Come, Emmanuel

O come, O come, Emmanuel,
And ransom captive Israel,
That mourns in lonely exile here
Until the Son of God appear.

Refrain:
Rejoice! Rejoice!
Emmanuel shall come to thee, O Israel.

O come, thou Wisdom from on high,
Who order all things far and nigh;
To us the path of knowledge show,
And teach us in her ways to go.
[Refrain]

O come, thou Day-spring, come and cheer
Our spirits by thine advent here;
Disperse the gloomy clouds of night,
And death's dark shadows put to flight.
[Refrain]

O come, O come, great Lord of might,
Who to thy tribes on Sinai's height
In ancient times once gave the law
In cloud and majesty and awe.
[Refrain]

O come, Desire of nations, bind
In one the hearts of all mankind;
Bid thou our sad divisions cease,
And be thyself our King of Peace.

—ANONYMOUS, twelfth century,
translated from Latin by John Mason Neale,
1851

ADULT CHALLENGE

Reflect on the differences in your behaviors, attitude, and language when you are in public compared to when you are in the privacy of your home. Would Jesus approve of both behaviors? Write the inconsistencies on a sheet of paper and pray over them. Then ask God to make you more whole in every situation, private or public.

CHILD PROMPT

Some days I know Jesus is disappointed when I _____

_____

_____

Day 6

Belief in the Mission

READ

Mark 1:1–8

KEY VERSES

And this was his message: "After me will come one more powerful than I, the thongs of whose sandals I am not worthy to stoop down and untie. I baptize you with water, but he will baptize you with the Holy Spirit." (Mk. 1:7–8)

Thirty-plus years out of high school, I began to attend college. The decision came with excitement yet much apprehension. I had the usual questions any student would have: Will I fit in? Will I be able to do the work? What kinds of people will I meet? In addition to the normal trepidations, I added my age, lack of experience, and lack of knowledge. I wanted to go but I was terrified!

My family and close friends had more faith in me than I did. My children promised to help me in those areas in which I was behind, and my husband offered support as well. Even with this, I wasn't sure I would succeed. There was only one thing left to do: pray! "Lord," I said, "if this is meant to be, then give me strength to succeed." I have succeeded, and I believe God has a plan. I haven't a clue what it is, but in his time I will find out.

When John the Baptist came on the scene 2,000 years ago, he believed the Messiah was coming. He lived a humble life away from any of the comforts of his day. His clothes were made from camel hair and his food was mainly locusts. Still, he exemplified the way to Christ. It is a road that is not easy, but filled with difficulties and hardships. People of John the Baptist's time thought he was strange and "had issues," as we would say now. There were those who must have asked: Where does he fit in? What is he doing? Is he really a man of God? Where did he come from?

Unlike my doubts about my "mission," John didn't have any doubt. He knew he *was* different from other people. He knew he *didn't* fit in. He had faith and believed, with all that he was, that Jesus was coming. He believed Jesus was God's Son. God had a plan. John would be his messenger, and because John believed, many repented and believed.

CONSIDER

1. Have you ever done something you didn't totally believe in?

2. How would you react to John the Baptist if he came today?

FAMILY ACTIVITY
Make gingerbread cookies

A German tradition for Christmas includes making gingerbread cookies and houses. Family nights are set aside for making the special cookies, as well as making gifts and decorations. Carry on the German tradition of baking gingerbread cookies by spending a special evening together in the kitchen.

Gingerbread Cookies

4 ounces	butter
4 ounces	vegetable shortening
1/4 cup	sugar
1/2 cup	firmly packed brown sugar
1/2 cup	molasses
1	large egg
2 1/4 cups	all-purpose flour
1 cup	whole-wheat flour
2 teaspoons	ground ginger
1 1/4 teaspoons	ground cinnamon
1 teaspoon	baking soda
1/4 teaspoon	ground nutmeg
1/4 teaspoon	ground cloves
1/8 teaspoon	salt

Preheat oven to 350°F. Coat pans lightly with cooking spray.

Cream butter and shortening with mixer on high 3 minutes or until soft. Beat in sugar. Continue beating 2 minutes until light and fluffy. Beat in molasses and then the egg, scraping down bowl twice.

Sift together flours, ginger, cinnamon, baking soda, nutmeg, cloves, and salt. Add dry ingredients to butter mixture in three batches, mixing just until each batch is blended. Shape into large flat ball by hand, kneading a few times until smooth. Shape into two flat circles. Wrap each circle in plastic wrap. Refrigerate a minimum of 2 hours or until firm enough to roll out.

Roll dough on lightly floured surface to 3/16-inch thickness. Cut shapes as desired, using gingerbread boy and girl cookie cutters or others of your choice. (Christmas bells or trees, wreaths, camels, and candy cane cutters are also good ideas.) Transfer to cookie sheets with a broad-angled spatula, leaving 1 inch between cookies.

Place similar size cookies on the same cookie sheet so they will all bake evenly. To make hanging ornaments, punch holes in the tops of shapes with a drinking straw.

Bake 9 1/2 to 12 minutes depending on the size of the cookies, rotating pans front to back once during baking. Edges should begin to brown and feel firm to the touch. Remove pans from oven. Transfer cookies to racks to cool completely. Be creative and decorate as desired.

You may choose to use hard candy decorations to add color to your creations or use a hard-drying frosting.

HARD-DRYING FROSTING

4 tablespoons	meringue powder
1 (16-ounce)	package powdered sugar (4 to 4 1/2 cups)
5-6 tablespoons	warm water
	assorted food coloring

Combine warm water and meringue powder in deep bowl; mix with electric mixer until foamy and powder has dissolved. Add powdered sugar and beat on low speed on mixer, until icing forms peaks; tint as desired with food coloring.

Note: Icing dries very quickly so keep bowl covered with plastic wrap.

After baking, place ribbons through the holes in the ornament cookies and tie a knot.

ADULT CHALLENGE

Imagine yourself as a modern-day John the Baptist. Does your life exemplify Christ's message of repentance, hope, and love? In what ways could your life do that?

CHILD PROMPT

If I were John the Baptist today, as God's messenger I would _____

_____

_____

Day 7

The Ultimate Gift

READ

Philippians 2:1–11

KEY VERSE

Do nothing out of selfish ambition or vain conceit, but in humility consider others better than yourselves. (Phil. 2:3)

I heard the story of a police officer who gave up his dream of being an astronaut because, as he told his son, "It was the right thing to do." In amazement the young teenager said, "But how could you give up your dream? There is nothing I wouldn't give to follow my dream." The father looked at his son with love and said, "I decided that this was more important."

Jesus knew what was important. As part of the Trinity, Jesus had existed since time began. Yet he knew when the time came, he would need to leave his Father and the Holy Spirit and become separate for a time. The separation must have been devastating as he hung on the cross. He felt so alone that he even asked the question, "My God, my God, why have you forsaken me?"

We have all been separated from someone we care about. It may be a close friend because of a move. It happens when dating couples separate, when death takes a loved one, or when divorce comes into the picture. Each of these instances causes pain, but when a

parent loses a child, the loss is nearly unbearable. When a child loses a parent, especially at a younger age, the healing process can take months, years, and sometimes a lifetime.

Yet, Jesus gave up his position in heaven as God to become a servant. He took on the form of a man and offered himself to take the lowest position known to man, knowing the agony he was sure to face. He lowered himself to the point of washing the feet of his disciples not long after James and John had been arguing about who was the greatest. He suffered physical pain and humiliation, but even this paled beside the agony of accepting the evil of this world as his own so that he could be the perfect, sinless sacrifice. This is the ultimate love story.

This act of love allows us to become children of God, so that one day we will spend eternity with God the Father, Jesus the Son, and the Holy Spirit. This is not only an amazing love story, it is the ultimate gift.

CONSIDER

1. What could you sacrifice for a person you love—this week? Perhaps in the coming year?
2. What could you sacrifice for Jesus? Could you sacrifice more of your time, your funds, your abilities?

FAMILY ACTIVITY
Create an Advent paper chain

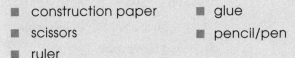

Christians living in China celebrate Christmas, known as the Holy Birth Festival, by decorating their homes with evergreens and a "tree of light" trimmed with lanterns and red paper chains to represent happiness.

Make your own paper chain to decorate your tree or some other place in your home. You may choose to use other colors besides red to celebrate your own happiness. The directions that follow give an added step to help celebrate this special season of Advent.

MATERIALS NEEDED

- construction paper
- scissors
- ruler
- glue
- pencil/pen

Cut seven strips of construction paper 8 inches by 1 inch in your chosen colors. Write on each strip one of the key verses from each of the seven days of this week. Glue the ends of one of the strips so they overlap to become a circle. Place a second strip inside the first; glue the ends to form another loop. Continue in this way until all seven strips have created a chain. Place this section of the chain on your tree or in other area for display.

You may choose to repeat this activity at the end of each week of Advent. Add the new section of seven strips to the previous section completed, with Scriptures from the past week written on them. Or you may choose to make the chain as long as you want the very first week.

While Shepherds Watched Their Flocks by Night

While shepherds watched their flocks
   by night,
All seated on the ground,
The angel of the Lord came down,
And glory shone around,
And glory shone around.

"Fear not!" said he, for mighty dread
Had seized their troubled mind.
"Glad tidings of great joy I bring
To you and all mankind
To you and all mankind.

"To you, in David's town, this day
Is born of David's line
A Savior, who is Christ the Lord,
And this shall be the sign,
And this shall be the sign.

"The heavenly babe you there shall find
To human view displayed,
All meanly wrapped in swathing bands,
And in a manger laid,
And in a manger laid.

"All glory be to God on high,
And to the Earth be peace;
Good will henceforth from Heaven to men
Begin and never cease,
Begin and never cease!"

—NAHUM TATE, 1700

ADULT CHALLENGE

How can you show love this Advent to someone you find it particularly difficult to be around? Pray that you can look past what seems to annoy you about this person to recognize their special gift. Then if possible, do something especially kind for this person.

CHILD PROMPT

I can show others they are important by _____

_____

_____

ADVENT

Week

2

Who Is Waiting?

Day 1

Ministers of the Faith

READE
Luke 1:67–79

KEY VERSES
And you, my child, will be called a prophet of the Most High; for you will go on before the Lord to prepare the way for him, to give his people the knowledge of salvation through the forgiveness of their sins. (Lk. 1:76–77)

As I read this passage from Luke, I am reminded of a pastor who said once to his congregation, "I am the pastor but we are all ministers of the faith." John the Baptist was given an extraordinary gift. He would be the forerunner of Jesus. He would be the one who proclaims the coming of the birth of Christ and lead many into the fold.

We do well to follow his example. We may not be the aggressive preacher, prolific writer, mesmerizing leader, or articulate teacher. We may be the quiet one in the pew who prays for each of these people. We may be the one who makes phone calls to the shut-ins to see how they are doing. The list of possible ministries is endless!

When our family made the difficult decision to put my mother-in-law into a nursing home, her Alzheimer's disease had reached a point where we were unable to give her the care she required. As her daughter conversed with the doctor, did the necessary paperwork, and made the proper phone calls, I stayed by my mother-in-law's side. I stroked her back and held her as she cried, unaware of where she even was. What I did was not grand. No one probably even noticed. But that's okay. At that moment, at that time, I needed to give my mother-in-law comfort and reassurance.

There are people every day in our lives who need consoling in some form. They need to be held and reassured that they are not alone. They need to know that Christ is the Messiah and can give them what we, as humans, cannot.

It is good for followers of Christ to share the love of Jesus when the opportunity presents itself, just as John the Baptist did. It may be in the form of preaching, teaching, or working with a youth group. It may simply come in the form of a prayer or a hug, giving comfort to someone who feels alone, grieving, lost, or forsaken.

CONSIDER

1. Have you ever been in a position where you gave of yourself and only God knew of your kindness? How did this make you feel?
2. What gift has God given you that best enables you to share your love of him?

FAMILY ACTIVITY
Place lighted candles in your windows

● ●

MATERIALS NEEDED

- candles in holders or electric "candles"
- appropriate Scriptures to be read
- or other materials chosen to add reverence to the occasion

As we continue getting ready for Christ's birth this Advent season, you may choose to place lighted candles in your windows to symbolize that Jesus came to be the Light of the World. Before lighting the candles (or plugging them in), choose Scriptures to be read at a particular window, or have a member or members of the family write a poem in honor of the event, or choose a person to say a special Christmas prayer as the light is lit. (Or you can do all three!) Several of the many Scriptures in the Bible that might be appropriate are John 8:12; John 12:35-36; John 1:1-9; and James 1:17. You may find different verses to your liking by using a Bible concordance or searching the Internet. (Enter the search terms "Scriptures Jesus Light of the World.")

You may choose to place fresh greenery around the candle base. Remember, if you're using real candles, make sure curtains or other material in the window are away from the flame, and keep small children a safe distance away. Blow out the candle flames before leaving the room.

O Come, All Ye Faithful

O come, all ye faithful,
Joyful and triumphant,
O come ye,
O come ye to Bethlehem;
Come and behold him
Born the King of angels;

Refrain:
O come, let us adore him,
O come, let us adore him,
O come, let us adore him,
Christ, the Lord.

Sing, choirs of angels,
Sing in exultation,
Sing, all ye citizens
of heaven above;
Glory to God,
Glory in the highest;
[Refrain]

Yea, Lord, we greet thee,
Born this happy morning,
Jesus, to thee be
all glory given;
Son of the Father,
Now in flesh appearing;
[Refrain]

—JOHN FRANCIS WADE, 1751

ADULT CHALLENGE

Think about the person who causes the most grief, anxiety, or frustration in your life. In what way can you show this person a special kindness, understanding, comfort, or love?

CHILD PROMPT

The person who annoys me the most is _____. I will try to be kind to that person by _____

_____

_____

Day 2

God Keeps His Promises

READ

Galatians 3:13–25

KEY VERSE

He redeemed us in order that the blessing given to Abraham might come to the Gentiles through Christ Jesus, so that by faith we might receive the promise of the Spirit. (Gal. 3:14)

People make promises every day. Some are simple statements between adults without any formality, but the promise is accepted and counted on. Some are made in frustration to a child in an effort to placate a given situation. Some promises are made with a single signature, which would prove ownership if needed. In human existence the most binding promises are those made before a court. To change anything within them is tedious, time-consuming, and often expensive.

God's promises aren't like any of the above. God promised Abraham that he, an old man, and his wife, a woman well beyond childbearing years, would have a son. This promise wasn't written on paper, there wasn't a handshake, and it wasn't heard before a court. Yet, as unlikely as such a situation seemed, God followed through on his promise in the birth of Isaac.

A Messiah was also promised many years ago. God didn't give many details of how the Messiah would come or when he would come, but God said a deliverer *would* come. Through the prophets, God described the Messiah's earthly lineage and even where he would be born. For many years the people waited. The prophets continued to give notice that the Messiah was coming. Many believed and many did not.

God kept that promise, as he has all others. He sent our Deliverer in the form of a baby. Those that believed recognized him. Others had expectations beyond what God promised. They thought surely the Messiah would come as a great king who would govern politically. But Jesus came as our King to rule our hearts, our minds, and our souls. We can "behold" him for all that he is. To "behold" him is to focus on him and occupy our minds so that all decisions and efforts in our daily life reflect him. This is a demonstration of faith. When we live for Jesus we are like Abraham, who believed that God's promises were real.

CONSIDER

1. Can you remember your last promise? Was it spoken or implied? Did you keep it?
2. Have you ever promised God something, perhaps in fear, frustration, or desperation? Did you keep your promise?

FAMILY ACTIVITY
Caroling at a nursing home or a hospital

Christmas is a wonderful, festive time of year. But for people who are in a nursing home or a hospital, Christmas can be sad and lonely. Christmas carols brighten and lift most people's spirits and moods. As a family, or a church group, arrange a date to visit a local nursing home or other health-care facility and sing carols to the residents. You can use musical instruments if you have them. The singing doesn't have to be perfect, and you will discover many of the patients will sing along, especially if you invite them to join in.

MATERIALS NEEDED

- lyrics to Christmas carols
- musical instruments (optional)
- happy voices!

After singing, take a few moments and visit with the residents. Often they enjoy seeing children and take great pleasure in just having a visitor. Pass the Christmas spirit on to those who may seem to have lost theirs.

● ●

We Three Kings

We three kings of Orient are,
bearing gifts we traverse afar
Field and fountain,
moor and mountain,
following yonder star.

Refrain:
O star of wonder, star of night,
star with royal beauty bright.
Westward leading, still proceeding,
Guide us to thy perfect light.

Born a King on Bethlehem's plain,
Gold I bring to crown him again
King forever, ceasing never
over us all to reign.
[Refrain]

Frankincense to offer have I,
incense owns a Deity nigh
Prayer and praising, all men raising,
Worship him, God most high.
[Refrain]

Glorious now behold him arise,
King and God and Sacrifice!
Alleluia, alleluia,
heaven to earth replies.
[Refrain]

—JOHN HENRY HOPKINS JR., 1857

ADULT CHALLENGE

People prayed for Jesus, their Messiah, to come for many years. This was their greatest wish. Write your greatest wish list of what you would like for every member of your family to receive and then write a wish list for yourself.

Name of Family Member	Wish	My Wishes for Myself

CHILD PROMPT

List two or three decisions and situations that you are facing this week. Then say to God, "I ask you, God, to help me with these things. I need you."

Day 3

A Silver Lining

READ

Micah 3:5–5:5

KEY VERSES

In the last days the mountain of the Lord's temple will be established as chief among the mountains; it will be raised above the hills, and peoples will stream to it. Many nations will come and say, "Come, let us go up to the mountain of the Lord, to the house of the God of Jacob. He will teach us his ways, so that we may walk in his paths." (Mic. 4:1–2a)

I believe that for every bad thing that happens, there is a good thing, too. Some people have suggested I have a "Pollyanna" attitude, an overwhelming optimism. When it comes to my faith, this may be true. God provides a "silver lining" behind every cloud.

In our everyday lives there are little things that just "happen" that frustrate us at the moment, but when we reflect upon them later, we can say, "If this hadn't happened, then this good thing wouldn't have, either."

For instance, have you ever found yourself five minutes late and discovered in your travel path, just moments before, there was an auto accident? Had you been on time, it could have been you. Another example is when you make a stressful move from one place to another, yet happily upon arrival you discover a church and a community that exactly meets your needs. If we pay attention, God will always show us the direction he wants us to go.

In our reading from Micah 3, we find that people veered away from God's plan and went in a different direction. Because of this, the prophet says, "Zion will be plowed like a field, Jerusalem will become a heap of rubble, the temple hill a mound overgrown with thickets." This is a desolate picture, but out of this awful occurrence, good surfaced. Out of this desolation came the promise of a Savior.

We now have the promise that anyone can be God's child and one day join him eternally. As we prepare for this Christmas season, it is our responsibility to respond to the "silver lining" God provided with love, enthusiasm, and joy.

CONSIDER

1. Are you or someone close to you going through a trial that seems especially difficult? Does the situation look hopeless? Ask God to show you how he intends to handle it. Ask, also, for grace, patience, and trust.

2. Have you ever been frustrated by situations beyond your control such as slow drivers, a flat tire, too much traffic, or other issues that made you late to where you were headed? How do you react to such situations?

FAMILY ACTIVITY
Create a family newsletter

As preparations continue during this Advent season, we find ourselves anxious and excited about buying and wrapping gifts and then having to wait. This is especially true for children. Sometimes we find that holiday preparations leave little time to reflect on the past year, with its growth, pain, dilemmas, expectations, disappointments, and achievements.

The best gift we can offer another, often, is our time. It's more difficult when family lives many miles away, friends are in another state, and loved ones may be in another country serving in the military. One way to share about the past year is to create a newsletter.

Rather than have one person compile the information, type it, and send it out, have each family member participate by writing part of the newsletter. Their entry should be whatever they choose as having been most relevant over the year. This may take some prompting and reminding of activities for young ones (and editing for the final copy). A child who cannot write can dictate to another sibling or a parent what she would like included in the newsletter. When editing, try to keep the words as near to the child's speaking as possible while making the meaning clear. In this manner the entry is really the child's own.

After all have contributed their "news," compile the information and send it via e-mail or through regular mail to people whom you haven't seen in a while. Be as creative as you can while sharing thoughts, poems, memories, achievements, and even heartaches. People enjoy reading about those they love. You may get such warm responses that you make this a new family tradition!

Go, Tell It on the Mountain

While shepherds kept their watching
Over silent flocks by night,
Behold throughout the heavens,
There shone a holy light:

Refrain:
Go, tell it on the mountain,
Over the hills and everywhere;
Go, tell it on the mountain
That Jesus Christ is born.

The shepherds feared and trembled
When lo! above the earth
Rang out the angel chorus
That hailed our Savior's birth:
[Refrain]

Down in a lowly manger
Our humble Christ was born
And God sent us salvation,
That blessed Christmas morn:
[Refrain]

When I was a seeker,
I sought both night and day;
I asked the Lord to help me,
And he showed me the way:
[Refrain]

He made me a watchman
Upon the city wall,
And if I am a Christian,
I am the least of all.
[Refrain]

—AFRICAN AMERICAN SPIRITUAL,
pre–1865

ADULT CHALLENGE

Consider a recent change that has caused you much uneasiness or anxiety. Write down all the problems with the situation. Write down the consequences of the change. Can you see God's silver lining? If not, bring your list before God and ask him to show you how this situation is better than the one you had been in or to show you the direction he wants you to take so you can see his plan.

CHILD PROMPT

The biggest frustration I face in school is _____

_____

I will ask God to help me to _____

_____

Day 4

To Be Like Mary

READ
Luke 1:26–38

KEY VERSE

"I am the Lord's servant," Mary answered. "May it be to me as you have said." Then the angel left her. (Lk. 1:38)

All of us have people we admire and look up to. Our children often use sports figures or other celebrities as their role models. From the baseball arena a child may say, "When I grow up I want to be just like Derek Jeter." Or from the basketball world, "I want to be just like Kobe Bryant." A budding actress might dream of being like Julia Roberts or Cameron Diaz. These people may or may not be your choice of models. You may prefer someone much less well known who has all the good qualities that these famous men and women do, in addition to others more relevant to your interests.

Role models have a significant impact on our children's lives. When our children admire people we have concerns about, we can offer alternatives. One such alternative would be Mary, the mother of our Savior.

When I think about how totally Mary accepted the word of God, I am in awe. Mary, a virgin, would give birth to the Messiah. She knew the social consequences of such an event. She would be seen as an "unwed mother." How would she tell her betrothed, Joseph, that she was already pregnant and convince him of what had happened? Certainly Joseph wasn't the child's biological father. Would he believe that this truly was God's plan?

The passage in Scripture doesn't indicate any hesitation. She accepted it as fact and said, "I am the Lord's servant. May it be to me as you have said." What power in her words. How I would like to be like Mary!

As we ready ourselves this Christmas season, we need to put ourselves in Mary's place. Do we read God's word and not hesitate, even for a moment, to apply it to our lives when it seems impossible to imagine? Do we look to God and say, "Whatever you want, Lord, here I am. Send me"? If we can, we begin an amazing journey. We may not be able to understand the importance, predict the outcome, or imagine the consequences, but if it is God's plan we will be able to follow through, just like Mary.

CONSIDER

1. Who was your role model as a child? Do you have a role model as an adult? What are the differences between the role model you chose as a child and the one you chose as an adult?

2. List the qualities you see important in a role model you would choose now. Do you see yourself meeting the criteria you deem important in the role model you would choose?

FAMILY ACTIVITY
Discover a role model ✩

Each person should choose a role model on whom to do research. (Children may require some help with direction if they don't have anyone in mind. They may choose a cartoon character or a hero who isn't real at all. This may provide the perfect opportunity to point this out or to let them discover it during their search. Encourage them to select a character from the Bible as their role model—or perhaps a contemporary Christian "hero.")

MATERIALS NEEDED

Research resources (Internet, library, etc.); a photograph of the chosen role model, scissors, glue, construction paper, cutout images to depict "favorites" of the chosen role model, and a Bible. For one wanting to focus on Mary, see the following Scriptures: Matthew 1-2, 12:46-50, 13:53-58; Mark 6:1-6; Luke 1-3, 8:19-21, 11:27-28, 24:1-11; John 1:1-18, 2:1-12, 19:17-42, 20:1-18; and Acts 1:1-14.

Locate a photograph of the admired person and glue it to a piece of construction paper. As you glean more information, add on other pieces of paper and glue each attractively to the original with the photograph.

Find out the following: What seems to matter most to your role model? What sort of person is he or she? How does he spend his free time? What sort of work does she do in the world? Are there instances you can find where she has gone out of her way to help others? Add any other information that is relevant to describing what kind of person this role model might be.

How Far Is It to Bethlehem?

How far is it to Bethlehem? Not very far.
Shall we find the stable room lit by a star?

Can we see the little Child? Is he within?
If we lift the wooden latch, may we go in?

May we stroke the creatures there, ox, ass, or sheep?
May we peek like them and see Jesus asleep?

Great kings have precious gifts, and we have nought,
Little smiles and little tears are all we brought.

For all weary children, Mary must weep.
Here, on his bed of straw, sleep, children, sleep.

God in his mother's arms, babe in the byre
Sleep, as they sleep who find their heart's desire.

—FRANCES ALICE CHESTERTON, early twentieth century

ADULT CHALLENGE

Write a letter to your role model telling him or her why you chose that individual. Be as specific as possible. You need not send the letter but pray for the person to whom you just wrote. Does this person live a godly life? Would you encourage other people to look to this person as a role model? Why or why not? What can you do to support this person?

CHILD PROMPT

My favorite actor, actress, or sports figure is _____.

My favorite role model is _____.

I like this person the best because _____.

Day 5

Sharing the News

READ
Luke 1:39–56

KEY VERSES
And Mary said: "My soul glorifies the Lord and my spirit rejoices in God my Savior, for he has been mindful of the humble state of his servant." (Lk. 1:46–48a)

My daughter received some exciting news recently but was asked to "keep it quiet." Since she could not yet share it with friends or coworkers, she came to me. She knew I would not share the information with anyone else, yet I would provide an avenue to express how happy she was.

Mary must have been thrilled with the information she received from the angel of the Lord, yet wondered what she would do with the information. News that important and exciting could not remain contained within the confines of one person. Surely she wondered not only with whom should she share it, but also if that person would think she was imagining such things. God provided the answer for her when the angel told her that her cousin Elizabeth was also with child. God knew Mary would need someone.

If God sent you important news, what would you do with the information? With whom would you share it? It's easy to share stories with those you know. But what about something your friend would consider eccentric? Suppose, after being in the business world for many years, you realized God was calling you to preach. Whom would you tell? Would you be comfortable telling your spouse, your coworkers, your neighbors, or even your extended family? There's no question each one would have a reaction. Would you believe strongly enough in God's direction to follow where he leads?

We *all* have important, exciting news to share. It may not seem as dramatic as changing careers. Nonetheless, it is important in our everyday lives and just as vital from a Christian perspective. We have the good news of Jesus' birth. As we continue our journey within this Advent season, look at the people around you—your neighbors, coworkers, family, or fellow students. Surely there is someone who needs to know your "good news." God's news is no secret. He wants us to be excited and share our joy with everyone we know.

CONSIDER

1. Have you ever had a secret you had to share with someone? How did you decide with whom to share it? What was the reaction to your news?

2. Have you ever been someone's confidant? How did you handle the situation? If you could do it over again, is there anything you might do or say differently?

FAMILY ACTIVITY
Make St. Lucia bread

• •

December 13 honors St. Lucia (Lucia is Latin for "Lucy") in the Swedish Christmas tradition. One version of the celebration describes the oldest daughter of each family dressing in a special white costume and treating her family with coffee and St. Lucia buns; others suggest it's the youngest daughter. In any case the daughter emulates the kindness of this early fourth-century saint who was martyred for her beliefs. It is believed the young woman wore candles in a wreath on her head to light her way while supplying food for Christians who were hiding in underground passageways.

Your family can make St. Lucia bread in her honor and follow the "role model" activity above to find out what makes St. Lucia so special.

Braided St. Lucia Bread

DOUGH

1/2 cup	water
2 (1/4-ounce)	packages active dry yeast
1 cup	milk
6 tablespoons	butter, cut in pieces
2	large eggs
1/4 cup	orange juice
1 tablespoon	grated orange rind
1/8 teaspoon	powdered saffron (optional)
1/3 cup	sugar
1/4 teaspoon	salt
1 cup	whole-wheat flour
4 1/2 – 5 1/2 cups	all-purpose flour

GLAZE
3 cups   confectioner's sugar
2-4 tablespoons   orange juice

GARNISH
½ cup   raisins

Dissolve the yeast in ½ cup warm water in a large bowl. Let it rest 5 minutes. Melt the butter in 1 cup of milk and add the mixture to the large bowl with the yeast mixture. In a separate bowl, beat the eggs, ¼ cup orange juice, orange rind, saffron, sugar, and salt until well mixed. Add to the large bowl. Mix in the 1 cup of wheat flour. Stir in the remaining flour, 1 cup at a time, until the dough is easy to handle. Turn the dough onto a floured surface and knead, adding enough flour as you work, until the dough is smooth and elastic. Place the dough in a greased bowl; cover and let rise until double in size. Punch down. Knead again. Divide the dough into three equal sections.

Roll each section lengthwise into a long rope that will make about a 12-inch circle when joined in a round. Braid the ropes together and transfer to a greased baking sheet. Bring the ends together to form a circle and pinch the ends together. Place the raisins throughout the braid sections. Allow the braid to rise until doubled, about one hour. Bake 25 minutes at 375 degrees Fahrenheit or until golden brown. Remove from the oven and allow to cool 20–25 minutes.

Mix the confectioner's sugar and 2-4 tablespoons orange juice until smooth and creamy. Drizzle over the bread. To complete the wreath, you may wish to place candles carefully on top in honor of St. Lucia.

ADULT CHALLENGE

Consider the ways you communicate your faith to those around you. How do you live your life differently because of your faith in Christ?

CHILD PROMPT

The best secret I ever told was ———————————————————————

The best secret I ever kept was ———————————————————————
(Do not feel you need to write the secret if it is *still* a secret and cannot be shared.)

Day 6

Waiting for the Treasure

READ

Luke 2:25–35

KEY VERSES

Simeon took him in his arms and praised God, saying: "Sovereign Lord, as you have promised, you now dismiss your servant in peace. For my eyes have seen your salvation, which you have prepared in the sight of all people, a light for revelation to the Gentiles and for glory to your people Israel." (Lk. 2:28–32)

When my daughter was almost four, she eagerly anticipated Christmas. She had asked for only one thing: a Cabbage Patch doll. That was the year, however, that all little girls wanted one. They were hard to find: stores sold out as soon as they arrived! Since it was the only thing she asked for, my husband and I searched and searched for this doll. We just couldn't find one, and we couldn't afford what the scalpers were asking.

On Christmas morning the children all opened their gifts with excitement. Each one brought sounds of pleasure. Finally it was time for clean up and a bit of organization. I found my youngest daughter sitting on the sofa later looking forlorn and sad. I asked what was wrong. Looking up at me, her big brown eyes sad, she said simply, "I didn't get a Cabbage Patch doll." I felt awful! My husband and I began anew, searching for a Cabbage Patch doll. We found one some weeks later, and when my little girl saw her treasure, she was filled with joy beyond belief. The doll became her companion for years.

Simeon was a righteous and devout man who also waited, with great expectation. Over his lifetime he must have seen many firstborn male children come into the temple to be consecrated, as this was the law of the Lord in that time. But when Mary and Joseph came in with baby Jesus, this was different, and Simeon knew it. He felt something special. This was the Christ. Can you imagine the thrill Simeon experienced when he held that child, knowing this was the One for whom he waited? His heart must have been full of an indescribable joy.

Do we respond like Simeon? Are we Christians excited about the birth of Christ? Are our hearts full and at peace? Do we have an indescribable joy?

Just as my small daughter experienced the thrill of receiving a treasure she longed for, we have received a treasure much greater. My daughter grew up and lost the "need" for the doll. We never "grow up" so much that we don't need Jesus. In fact, as we grow, our need for him grows stronger. It is he who guides us through this life on earth. His promises are sure and his love is pure. There is no greater gift this Advent season.

CONSIDER

1. Have you ever wanted a gift so badly you could hardly contain yourself? Did you ever get your treasure? Was it worth the wait?

2. Have you ever given a gift to someone you knew wanted the item really badly? How did you present the gift? What was his or her reaction? How did it make you feel?

"Service of the Heart" Puzzle ☆ ✯★

Mary's service to the Lord was "of the heart." She was thrilled to be asked to serve her Lord. We should follow her example! Often we are afraid or intimidated by what God asks us to do. Mary knew she was called to do something special. Use the numbered letters of the words "Service of the Heart" as your code to fill in the missing letters from the passage found in Luke 1. And then search your heart to see if God is leading you to a special "service of the heart."

S E R V I C E	O F	T H E	H E A R T
1 2 3 4 5 6	7 8	9 10	11

"_ _M _ _ _ L_ _D_ _ _ _ _ _N_."
5 11   9 10 2   7 3 1   1 2 3 4 11 9

M_ _ _Y _N_W_ _ _ _D. "M_Y _ _ B_
11 3   11 1 2 3 2   11   5 9   2

_ _ M_ _ _ Y_U _ _ _ _ _ _ _D,"
9 7   2   11 1   7   10 11 4 2   1 11 5

_ _ _ _N _ _ _ _ _NG_L L_ _ _ _ _ _ _.
9 10 2   9 10 2   11 2   2 8 9   10 2 3

from Luke 1

Find the answer on page 151.

Come, Thou Long-Expected Jesus

Come, thou long-expected Jesus,
Born to set thy people free;
From our fears and sins release us;
Let us find our rest in thee.
Israel's Strength and Consolation,
Hope of all the earth thou art;
Dear Desire of every nation,
Joy of every longing heart.
Born thy people to deliver,

Born a child and yet a King,
Born to reign in us forever,
Now thy gracious kingdom bring.
By thine own eternal Spirit
Rule in all our hearts alone;
By thine all sufficient merit,
Raise us to thy glorious throne.

—CHARLES WESLEY, 1745

ADULT CHALLENGE

Consider all your friends, family, and acquaintances. Are any of them in greater need than you? What gift could you give them that extends Christ's love? It may be food, shelter, time, or another kindness. Once you choose a person (or family) with whom to share blessings, carry out a plan that will let the light of God's love shine.

CHILD PROMPT

_____ probably won't have as nice a Christmas as I will. This week I will give him/her a gift of _____ _____ to share a kindness and demonstrate Jesus' love.

Day 7

Bird Songs

READ
Isaiah 49:1–13

KEY VERSES
"I will also make you a light for the Gentiles, that you may bring my salvation to the ends of the earth." . . . Shout for joy, O heavens; rejoice, O earth; burst into song, O mountains! For the Lord comforts his people and will have compassion on his afflicted ones. (Isa. 49:6b, 13)

My friend had an awful morning one summer where everything seemed to go wrong. She was running late when she arrived to pick me up, and when she reached to adjust her rearview mirror, it promptly fell off. The car started overheating, we got snarled in road construction, and finally, in the sweltering temperature, we had to turn the heater on so the fan would run, because the temperature light came on as we waited in traffic! Sitting in the seat beside her, I found all I could do was laugh! The situation had reached a point where being upset wasn't going to work.

Later in the morning a coworker looked at her and said, "Your hair looks so nice today!" She responded, "It's my running-late, heater-on, window-open, windblown look!" She, of course, had to laugh too. Life often upsets us. Things don't merely go wrong—on occasion they go from bad to worse! Singing and shouting for joy are the last things we want to do.

Nature has a way of putting life in perspective. Birds sing no matter what the weather. Whether in rain, snow, or intense heat, they still sing. We humans are a little like the birds, in that when we are happy we often want to sing. Our joy must be heard. Little children, when happy, will often burst into song. Sometimes we find ourselves humming a tune before we realize it, but only when things are good. When things are going wrong, we can't pull up a single note of a song. More often we react with tears.

Our Scripture today promises, years before the actual occurrence, that Jesus would come to be "a light for the Gentiles . . . salvation to the ends of the earth." That is reason for rejoicing even when things don't seem to be going our way. We were promised the gift of salvation because God loved us enough to sacrifice his Son. We have much to be happy about! All we need do is believe. While you wait on him this Advent season, remember that your joy comes from him. Joy can be found in all circumstances, even if it's hidden for a while.

CONSIDER

1. How did you handle the situation the last time you had several things go wrong all at one time? What might you do differently the next time?
2. Have you ever been someone else's "silver lining"? When was the last time you encouraged someone with an unexpected compliment or greeting?

FAMILY ACTIVITY
String popcorn for your Christmas tree

Franklin Pierce, the fourteenth president of the United States, introduced the first Christmas tree to the White House in 1856. The ornamentation likely included popcorn strings. So, pop some kernels and decorate your tree in this American family tradition!

Pop unbuttered popcorn of your choice (by air, microwave, or traditional pan style). Allow the popcorn to get stale by leaving it out in the air for several hours or overnight. Thread a needle with heavy thread and tie a knot on the long end. Poke a hole in a kernel of popcorn with the needle and carefully move the popcorn on the string to the knot. Add another piece of popcorn and another and another until the thread is nearly filled. Remove the needle and knot that end near the last piece of popcorn. Begin another string until you are out of popcorn! Trim your tree with this special decoration.

ADULT CHALLENGE
What do you have to be happy about, right now? This year? As you look forward to next year? Write these things down and put them in your Bible or somewhere else where you will see them regularly.

CHILD PROMPT
My last bad day was _____

_____.

The "silver lining" of that day was _____

_____.

3

Why Are
We Waiting?

Day 1

God's Blueprint

READ

Isaiah 62

KEY VERSES

For Zion's sake I will not keep silent, for Jerusalem's sake I will not remain quiet, till her righteousness shines out like the dawn, her salvation like a blazing torch. . . . As a young man marries a maiden, so will your sons marry you; as a bridegroom rejoices over his bride, so will your God rejoice over you. . . . The Lord has made proclamation to the ends of the earth: "Say to the Daughter of Zion, 'See, your Savior comes! See, his reward is with him, and his recompense accompanies him.'" (Isa. 62:1, 5, 11)

I heard the story recently of a young man whose middle name was Godfield. As a child, he disliked his name. Admittedly, it is not a name you hear often, but this young man was so named because his mother was convinced the child she carried had a special calling from God. He would one day be in the "field" working for the Savior. As a teen he wasn't interested in any such idea. Still his mother persisted in her belief and insisted on reminding him from time to time.

God works in all our lives, even when we're not noticing. Despite this young man's best efforts to find meaning elsewhere during his younger years, he now finds himself doing just what he heard about over and over in his life—he's a missionary. And he loves his middle name! His mother's hope has indeed come to fruition.

Our Scripture is much the same. The prophet knew God had a plan. He knew one day a Messiah would come to claim his people. The prophet said he wouldn't be quiet until what he knew would happen had come to pass. He was convinced that if he kept repeating it, people would believe. The Messiah would come! He would cure them of their sin and set them apart for God.

As believers, we still have the need of being reminded that God has a design for each of his children, a blueprint for our lives. We can be like the young man who didn't like his name and took many years to recognize God's will for his life. Or, as we prepare our hearts this Advent season, we can recognize that we need to be in tune with God's will, ask for his plan to be revealed to us, and then follow the blueprint he has designed.

CONSIDER

1. Blueprints are typically made for new homes. Have you ever considered that your life is a blueprint designed by God? Have you ever wanted something different in your life from where you are now?

2. Have you ever been so convinced of something you would not leave a situation alone until you found the answers? Did you try talking to God about it?

FAMILY ACTIVITY
Wrap gifts as a family

Some people consider gift wrapping a chore. Others enjoy the process of cutting, folding, taping, and ribbon tying as an expression of who they are. In many families it is the job of a single person, or perhaps two, to wrap the gifts, especially if the children of the family are very young. They may not have the finger dexterity or the ability to cut with scissors to do the job well. Yet often, children thrill at the chance to help with wrapping.

This year, wrap your gifts together as a family. Make a special snack and hot chocolate (or another favorite) while Christmas music is playing to create a festive occasion. Allow the child to tear off pieces of tape or hold her finger on the ribbon firmly in place while the adult ties. The child can help with placing the bows on the finished gift. If you haven't used your handmade wrapping paper, this might be just the time. Share stories of Christmases past and allow the child to share his anticipation of the arrival of the Christ Child.

Just as God has a blueprint for our lives, he has plans for our families to spend time together. The gift may not be perfectly wrapped with all the "extra" help, but you will have nurtured the family spirit. This is more important than all the perfectly wrapped presents in the world!

Good Christian Men, Rejoice

Good Christian men, rejoice
With heart and soul and voice;
Give ye heed to what we say:
News! News!
Jesus Christ is born today:
Ox and ass before him bow
And he is in the manger now.
Christ is born today!
Christ is born today!

Good Christian men, rejoice
With heart and soul and voice;
Now ye hear of endless bliss;
Joy! Joy!
Jesus Christ was born for this!
He has ope'd the heav'nly door

And man is blessed evermore.
Christ was born for this!
Christ was born for this!

Good Christian men, rejoice
With heart and soul and voice;
Now ye need not fear the grave;
Peace! Peace!
Jesus Christ was born to save!
Calls you one and calls you all
To gain his everlasting hall.
Christ was born to save!
Christ was born to save!

—JOHN MASON NEALE,
mid-nineteenth century

ADULT CHALLENGE

Consider your "plan" for your life. Is your life what you wanted or planned? Do you have regrets? Ask God to show you if you are where you should be.

CHILD PROMPT

If I could have any other name, I would choose _____ because _____.

Day 2

A Different Kind of Peace

READ

John 14:23–31

KEY VERSE

Peace I leave with you; my peace I give you. I do not give to you as the world gives. Do not let your hearts be troubled and do not be afraid. (Jn. 14:27)

I recently entered the college scene after thirty-one years of marriage and five grown children. It has been a wonderful experience, at times frustrating and challenging. There are days when I'm overwhelmed with homework and exhaustion. My retired husband has been wonderful with the change in our lifestyle, but I still feel the strain. This has completely altered what we *planned* to do once we retired!

The other night I had a dream in which the stress of college was almost unbearable. I woke agonizing over my responsibilities and wondered if it was all worth it. Should I be there at all? I questioned, unable to go back to sleep. Why am I doing this? Why am I putting myself through the extra stress and exertion of school when life is already full? After tossing and turning for a bit I went to the Lord in prayer. I'd long believed this was God's plan. I hadn't a clue what he'd do with my prayer, but still I prayed.

In the morning I was amazed at how peaceful I felt. I *knew* without a doubt I was where I was supposed to be at that moment. I was comfortable picking up my books and studying, confident that God would be with me. I *knew* this peace could only come from God.

Sometimes it's hard to understand what's going on around us. Situations arise in life where we must make hard decisions. Issues cause our minds to turn in other directions in fear of the unknown. How can we be certain we are doing the right thing? There is only one place to get the answers.

Jesus promised to be with us. He comforts us when we get rattled. He calms our fears. When we call on his name our fears can be squelched, our minds can become at ease, and our souls can rest.

Whatever you are facing this Advent season, call on the Prince of Peace. Only he can give us the gift of peace that passes understanding and cause our hearts not to be troubled.

CONSIDER

1. Do you consider yourself a strong person? Are you decisive and passionate regarding your values and direction in life? What causes you to waver?

2. Have you ever been in a situation where you wondered if you were doing the right thing? Did worry nearly overwhelm you? How did you work though it?

Star Code Puzzle

Jesus is all that is good and honorable. He is the Good Shepherd and he is the Morning Star. He is always there to light our way if we ask and allow him. Use the "star code" to find the Scripture verse from Revelation 22. Notice that you are given one number for three letters (except for two stars where there are only two). You must choose which letter to use.

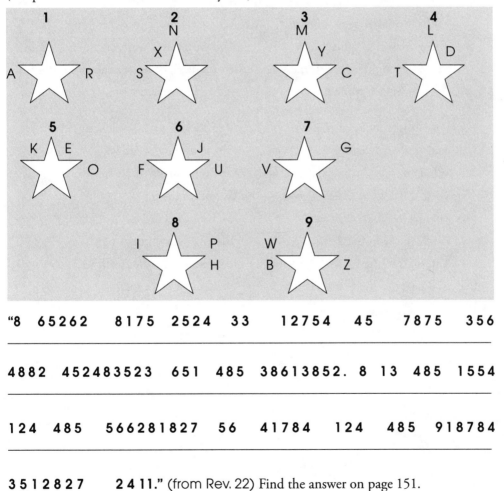

"8   65262   8175   2524   33   12754   45   7875   356

_____

4882   452483523   651   485   38613852.   8   13   485   1554

_____

124   485   566281827   56   41784   124   485   918784

_____

3512827   2411." (from Rev. 22) Find the answer on page 151.

_____

O Little Town of Bethlehem

O little town of Bethlehem,
How still we see thee lie.
Above thy deep and dreamless sleep
The silent stars go by;
Yet in thy dark streets shineth
The everlasting Light;
The hopes and fears of all the years
Are met in thee tonight.

For Christ is born of Mary,
And, gathered all above
While mortals sleep, the angels keep
Their watch of wondering love.
O morning stars, together
Proclaim the holy birth.
And praises sing to God the King.
And peace to men on earth.

Where children, pure and happy,
Pray to the Blessed Child;
Where misery cries out to thee,
Son of the Mother mild;
Where charity stands watching,
And faith holds wide the door,
The dark night wakes, the glory breaks,
and Christmas comes once more.

O Holy Child of Bethlehem,
Descend to us, we pray;
Cast out our sin and enter in;
Be born in us today!
We hear the Christmas angels
The great glad tidings tell;
O come to us, abide with us,
Our Lord Emmanuel!

—PHILLIPS BROOKS, 1868

ADULT CHALLENGE

Write down some of the worries you are faced with, being as specific as possible. These could include marriage, children, finances, career, education, or any number of issues. Place your list in your car or somewhere near your bedside. Look at it frequently. Accept God's peace.

CHILD PROMPT

I worry about _____

_____

I am going to ask God to _____

_____ about this problem.

Day 3

Making Choices

READ
Hebrews 10:1-10

KEY VERSES
First he said, "Sacrifices and offerings, burnt offerings and sin offerings you did not desire, nor were you pleased with them" (although the law required them to be made). Then he said, "Here I am, I have come to do your will." He sets aside the first to establish the second. And by that will, we have been made holy through the sacrifice of the body of Jesus Christ once for all. (Heb. 10:8-10)

Choices can be difficult. My youngest son thought he knew what he wanted to do when he graduated from college—that is, until he changed his mind. He's searching, as are many other young people. But they aren't the only ones in that dilemma. We are searching as a nation, as well. Some of this searching can be healthy, but as we've seen recently, other behaviors such as greed and selfishness can lead us into trouble financially, socially, and spiritually.

Jesus came to replace the old ways. He came to be the one and only holy sacrifice so we would be free from sin. He provided a way for us to be forgiven once and for all. Jesus came freely and willingly to die on a cross so that my sins could be forgiven. Further, his sacrifice wasn't just for *me*, it was for every single person who would make the choice to serve him.

Choices can be difficult. It's a lifetime challenge to make the right choices. The greatest challenge, the one that means more than anything else, is the choice to follow Christ.

CONSIDER

1. What do you consider your greatest decision? Was this also your most difficult?
2. Have you ever made a decision that you've later regretted? How did you come to see what you should have done?

FAMILY ACTIVITY
Ask the question "What if?"

Christmas is a time when children are beside themselves with wonder and anticipation. They are in awe of the lights, the tree, decorations, shopping, wrapping, baking, and everything Christmas represents. Adults can be filled with this same awe, if they allow themselves to be, but from a different "grown-up" perspective.

Slow down from all the preparations and festivities, gather the family around the tree or another familiar area, and ask the question, "What if?"

What if Mary hadn't agreed to be God's servant?
What if Joseph hadn't listened to the angel and no longer wanted Mary as his bride?
What if the innkeeper had allowed them a room at the inn?
What if the angels hadn't announced Jesus' birth to the shepherds?
What if Herod had found the baby Jesus before his family escaped to Egypt?
What if God hadn't sent his Son to redeem us from our sin?

There are many more "what if" questions that your family can discuss to generate conversation. Invite the young ones in your home to ask questions of their own.

• •

I Heard the Bells on Christmas Day

I heard the bells on Christmas Day
Their old familiar carols play,
And wild and sweet the words repeat
Of peace on earth, good will to men.

I thought how, as the day had come,
The belfries of all Christendom
Had rolled along the unbroken song
Of peace on earth, good will to men.

And in despair I bowed my head:
"There is no peace on earth," I said,
"For hate is strong and mocks the song
Of peace on earth, good will to men."

Then pealed the bells more loud and deep:
"God is not dead, nor doth he sleep;
The wrong shall fail, the right prevail,
With peace on earth, good will to men."

Till, ringing, singing, on its way,
The world revolved from night to day,
A voice, a chime, a chant sublime,
Of peace on earth, good will to men!

—HENRY WADSWORTH LONGFELLOW, 1867

ADULT CHALLENGE

Choose a topic from the Bible that interests you. Select a word or a phrase—perhaps "faithfulness," "sacrifice," or "love." Next, begin to search the Bible using a concordance, or discuss with your pastor or Bible study class, to see what God says specifically about your topic. Pray about your findings. Decide if there is something specific you can do to embrace God's teaching first within the confines of your family, and then within your community.

CHILD PROMPT

Sometimes I wonder, what if I were to _____

_____.

Day 4

Use the Calculator!

READ

Titus 2:11–14

KEY VERSES

For the grace of God that brings salvation has appeared to all men ... while we wait for the blessed hope—the glorious appearing of our great God and Savior, Jesus Christ. (Titus 2:11, 13)

I had exams yesterday in two of my college classes. I underwent extreme levels of stress before the tests while preparing and then again afterward worrying about how I performed. I left both classes unsure of my simple goal: "Just do your best." My son is taking the same mathematics class, and as I lay in bed early this morning, still thinking about the test and the results, I thought, "Dave will do fine. He'll just use the calculator!"

At that point I felt so ridiculous. The first problem on the test really unnerved me. I *knew* how to put the problem in the calculator just as Dave does, but instead of doing it, I worked the entire problem out by hand. It took much longer, causing me further stress because I was concerned about doing the process right, and it didn't ensure the correct answer!

When Jesus came as a small baby, he wasn't recognized for what he was. He brought salvation to the world. Yet even when he began teaching as an adult, many still didn't recognize that he was their salvation, the answer to their problems.

Christian people today often still try "to go it alone." We rely on ourselves to find the answers. We wear ourselves out needlessly, simply because we didn't go to the Lord in prayer. Not only have we worn ourselves out, we're often not sure we've done the right thing! How could we miss something so obvious? I asked myself the same thing this morning concerning my math test. I had my calculator right on the table beside me.

As we wait "for the blessed hope—the glorious appearing of our great God and Savior, Jesus Christ," we need to remember God is with us always. We often forget that in our day-to-day lives. He will comfort us, guide us, and help us with all we ask—but we have to follow.

CONSIDER

1. Do you find yourself trying to be in control of situations that ultimately are beyond your control? Have you lost sleep, cried tears, or worried yourself sick (physically, in some cases) over issues where you simply feel inept or useless?

2. Have you considered that if you had given the situation over to God before you became frustrated, you might have replaced the exhaustion of the overwhelming problem with God's peace long before the circumstances threatened to defeat you?

FAMILY ACTIVITY
Go through toys and give "hardly used" items to a church or a community organization ✩

As Christmas approaches, reflect with your family on all the blessings you have. This may include health, home, family, church, and the material things we find in our closets in the way of clothes or other items. For children, the items may be toys they have outgrown or used a time or two and set aside.

Locate a church or a community organization to donate your gifts to. As you go through the items to donate, check to determine if they are in poor, good, or excellent condition. Explain to the kids that it's not a true gift to give only your "poor condition" items. True giving means giving what is valuable to us. Wrap your good or excellent items for children who could use them. Check with the facility you have chosen for what is required on each label. It may be a name, or it may be "girl" or "boy" with the preferred age.

Give a less than fortunate child a happier Christmas this year. Share from your abundance.

God Rest Ye Merry, Gentlemen

God rest ye merry, gentlemen,
Let nothing you dismay;
Remember Christ, our Savior,
Was born on Christmas day,
To save us all from Satan's power
When we were gone astray.

Refrain:
O tidings of comfort and joy,
comfort and joy,
O tidings of comfort and joy.
From God our heavenly father,
A blessèd angel came;
And unto certain shepherds
Brought tidings of the same:
How that in Bethlehem was born
The Son of God by name.
[Refrain]

"Fear not," then said the angel,
"let nothing you affright,
This day is born a Savior
Of pure Virgin bright,
To free all those who trust in him
From Satan's power and might."
[Refrain]

The shepherds at those tidings
Rejoicèd much in mind,
And left their flocks a-feeding
In tempest, storm and wind,
And went to Bethlehem straightway,
This blessèd Babe to find.
[Refrain]

And when they came to Bethlehem
Where our dear Savior lay,
They found him in a manger,
Where oxen feed on hay;
His mother Mary kneeling down,
Unto the Lord did pray.
[Refrain]

Now to the Lord sing praises,
All you within this place,
And with true love and brotherhood
Each other now embrace;
This holy tide of Christmas
All other doth deface.
[Refrain]

—Unknown, fifteenth century

ADULT CHALLENGE

People facing problems sometimes become so overwhelmed by the issues that they also end up fighting depression. Do you know someone who is fighting depression? Pray today that God will touch their lives and bring peace. Send a card or a note simply saying "hello" and let them know you are thinking of them and praying for them.

CHILD PROMPT

I am giving (name of toy, here) _____ to a child who needs it more than I do. If I could talk with the child who receives this toy, I would tell him/her _____

_____

_____

_____.

Day 5

The Winner

READ

Philippians 4:8–19

KEY VERSES

Finally, brothers, whatever is true, whatever is noble, whatever is right, whatever is pure, whatever is lovely, whatever is admirable—if anything is excellent or praiseworthy—think about such things. Whatever you have learned or received or heard from me, or seen in me—put it into practice. And the God of peace will be with you. (Phil. 4:8–9)

The question was asked recently at a workshop I attended, "If the world ultimately had to choose either science or religion, which one would win?" A young man in the group was firm in the belief that science would win, while I and some others stood behind religion. "I need proof of things, concrete proof!" he said. "I do things for me that I decide, not what I am told from a book." Others countered that faith is where we get our morals; he responded, "But I do good things. I know right from wrong, but it's still up to me." Despite our efforts, we couldn't seem to explain that no matter how much good you do or how much you learn, you won't have peace.

Paul in the Scripture above was trying to make Christians see that when we think of "godly things" we will have God's peace. Until we have his peace, we will continue to search because we are born with a need for God. There is nothing on this earth that can replace God's peace. Science, with all its advancement and the good it has done for the world in technology, medicine, and modern conveniences, cannot give us what God does. Certainly there is satisfaction from a job well done or the success that comes from finding a cure for a devastating disease. But even this cannot bring us peace.

What we must remember is to keep everything in perspective. Our minds were created to search not only for those things that are for the good of humankind, but for those things that are for the good of our souls as well. This can be done only when our hearts are right with God.

I pray my young friend will one day realize he's not in control. Ultimately God is the Master of our lives. We must, as Paul pointed out, think about what is good and right, lovely and admirable, excellent and praiseworthy, and give God the credit. It is through him that we can find peace.

CONSIDER

1. If you were asked the question my young friend was asked—"If the world ultimately had to choose either science or religion, which one would win?"—how would you answer? More important, why do you choose your answer?

2. Do you know God's peace today? Is it easier—or harder—for you to feel God's peace at this time of year?

FAMILY ACTIVITY
Make holiday candleholders

Jesus came to be the "Light of the world," to provide salvation and a peace that cannot come from any other source. Make holiday candleholders as a reminder that he is the perfect Light. The candles can be used to decorate your home or as gifts for others.

MATERIALS NEEDED

- paper plates
- small glass baby food jars (infant or junior size) washed and dried
- liquid glue
- colored tissue paper
- ribbon
- a small votive candle
- a paint brush
- glitter and other decorations as desired

Each family member should have a paper plate and a small jar. The paper plate is used as the workspace. It will catch any drops of glue that might fall and any glitter that does not stick to the jar. Place the glue in a small container. Add drops of water to thin the glue. Tear or cut small pieces of the colored tissue paper. Using the paintbrush, apply a thin coat of glue to the outside of one side of the jar. Apply the pieces of tissue paper over the glue, overlapping in some areas. Apply a thin layer of glue to the other side of the jar and again place small pieces of tissue paper on top of the glue, overlapping when desired to create "new" colors. Apply glitter to the sticky areas (the glue will seep through the paper to feel sticky). Allow to dry. Apply several drops of glue (undiluted) around the outside of the neck of the jar. Place a ribbon over the wet glue. When it dries, cut the ribbon and keep it flat, or use a longer piece of ribbon and tie a small bow.

Place a small votive candle in the center of the jar. Light the candle and thank God for sending Jesus to become our "Light."

ADULT CHALLENGE

Select a recent scientific advancement or discovery. Inform yourself on at least the basics of it. Then, ask yourself: How can we use this to further God's kingdom?

CHILD PROMPT

The most fascinating thing I've learned in science is _____

_____

_____.

God would like this because _____.

Day 6

Like a Lightbulb

READ
Luke 24:36–49

KEY VERSES
Then he opened their minds so they could understand the Scriptures. He told them, "This is what is written: The Christ will suffer and rise from the dead on the third day, and repentance and forgiveness of sins will be preached in his name to all nations, beginning at Jerusalem." (Lk. 24:45–47)

I worked as a teacher's assistant for several years, a job that put me in direct contact with children who were struggling with the material being taught in class. It was my job to help them understand the lesson on a one-to-one basis. Sometimes it took repeated efforts—going over the material again and again—before the connection was made. It is exhilarating to see children finally grasp what they've struggled to understand. It's like a lightbulb turning on in their minds. Their faces light up with excitement and pleasure because they finally understand. This experience gives them the confidence to continue to the next immediate problem before them.

Jesus' disciples seem a little bit like the children I worked with. Their Master and friend had been taken from them, crucified, and buried. They didn't understand how such a thing could take place, even though Jesus had tried to warn them through his teachings that this would happen. They were downcast, sad, frustrated, and probably even angry. Then, amazingly, Jesus appeared to them, talked with them, showed them his nail-scarred hands and feet, and even ate with them. At first, this didn't make sense. They had seen him on the cross. They knew he had died and was placed in the tomb. They knew there was a stone in front of it, so that no one could take the body.

Again the question arises, *How could this happen?* The Scripture says Jesus "opened their minds." He provided a way for understanding. With this understanding came the mission before his disciples: go into all the nations and preach of salvation and life eternal.

Our personal "lightbulbs" come on when we study and search God's word, just like the child who must repeatedly go over the material in the classroom, sometimes even with additional help from someone more experienced. Each bit of knowledge gained through daily reading, prayer, and time spent alone with God provides the means for continued growth. This enables us to share what we've learned with others.

CONSIDER

1. Have you ever struggled to learn something, like biology, mathematics, a new language, or another subject? Did you become frustrated? How did you finally learn the material?
2. Does studying God's word seem overwhelming? If you took more time than usual to do it, during this season of Advent, what would you study?

FAMILY ACTIVITY

Make an idea box of what you would like to learn

Learning is a lifelong process. Make an idea box of things you would like to learn. (Each family member may choose to have their own box to make the process personal and deliberate.)

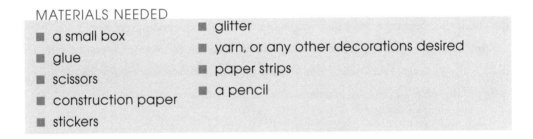

MATERIALS NEEDED

- a small box
- glue
- scissors
- construction paper
- stickers
- glitter
- yarn, or any other decorations desired
- paper strips
- a pencil

Find an unused small box with a lid. (The lid can be attached or come completely off—either will do.) An empty Christmas card box would work well. Begin by covering the box with construction paper. Add stickers, glitter, yarn, lace or any other decoration to make it uniquely yours. Be sure to cover the outer portion of the lid, as well. Write on each of the strips of paper the name of something you would like to learn or learn about over this next year. It may be a sport, a craft, music, a language, Bible verses, Bible people, sewing, geography, insects, weather patterns, family heritage, and so on—include anything you would find worth learning. Put your ideas in the box and close it. On a day when you are bored and feel like you have nothing to do, open the box and take one slip of paper out, and study whatever is written on it. Begin opening your mind and "turning on the lightbulb"!

ADULT CHALLENGE

Choose a book of the Bible that particularly frustrates you. Join a Bible study group or partner with someone who will share your journey of trying to understand this book in the coming year.

CHILD PROMPT

The most difficult subject in school is _____.
But I can tell I'm making progress because _____
_____
_____.

Day 7

Milestones

READ

Philippians 3:12–21

KEY VERSES

But our citizenship is in heaven. And we eagerly await a Savior from there, the Lord Jesus Christ, who, by the power that enables him to bring everything under his control, will transform our lowly bodies so that they will be like his glorious body. (Phil. 3:20–21)

I remember being excited as a child when I turned age eight. I don't remember why, but at the time it seemed important. Then I waited eagerly for age thirteen, then sixteen, followed by eighteen, and then twenty-one. All these ages have significance, as I watched the process repeated with my own children. Each is a marker of growth that has particular meaning. We mark milestones throughout our lives!

In our passage today, Paul talks about eagerly awaiting Christ's return. This has nothing to do with age but rather with a milestone in our Christian faith. Just as each milestone in our earthly life is reached with a certain amount of growing pains, the same remains true in our Christian faith.

We begin our walk by finding out who Jesus is and coming to know him. As we grow, we come to know the Holy Spirit and trust him enough to allow him to control our lives.

We continue to grow in prayer, Bible reading, and obedience. We reach a point of trust and belief and stewardship until finally we can discern God's will in our lives.

This isn't an easy process, any more than is maturing in our earthly lives. It takes work, dedication, falls and failures, and persistence! With determination we will reach the next goal. We must not let life's struggles get us down, but as Paul put it, we must "press on to take hold of that for which Christ Jesus took hold of me."

As we wait for Jesus this Advent season, let's reflect. Do we press onward, or have we stopped, unsure of why we are waiting? Do we know what we're waiting for, or have we forgotten in all the busyness of life? What have we done over the past year in preparation for Christ's return? Let us remember that Jesus' death and resurrection gives us hope and a reason to press on.

CONSIDER

1. What do you consider the greatest milestone in your life? Why?
   As you reflect on it, do you see its importance now as you did when you were approaching it?
2. Can you see milestones in your faith journey? Can you name them?
   Did these milestones come easily or was their achievement a struggle?

FAMILY ACTIVITY
Make Irish Christmas cookies

Christmas is primarily a religious holiday in Ireland, but the day includes family fun as well. Irish Christmas cookies are one example of the festive, family side of Christmas.

Irish Christmas Cookies

1 cup	butter, softened
1 cup	granulated sugar
3	large eggs
2 cups	all-purpose flour
1/4 cup	strong black coffee or strong tea
1/4 cup	candied citron, chopped
1/4 cup	golden raisins, chopped
1/4 cup	almonds, chopped

Preheat oven to 375 degrees Fahrenheit. Prepare two greased cookie sheets; set aside.

In a small mixing bowl, cream together butter and sugar. Beat in eggs until well blended. Add flour and coffee or tea, and beat dough until smooth. Add the fruit and nuts; mix well. Drop cookie dough from a tablespoon onto prepared cookie sheets.

Bake each sheet of cookies 8 to 10 minutes. Remove cookies from baking sheets with a spatula while still warm. Place on wire rack to cool. Store cookies in an airtight container, with a slice of white bread to maintain their soft, fruity texture.

O Come, Little Children

O come, little children, O come, one and all,
To Bethlehem's stable, in Bethlehem's stall.
And see with rejoicing this glorious sight,
Our Father in heaven has sent us this night.

Oh, see in the manger, in hallowèd light
A star throws its beam on this holiest sight.
In clean swaddling clothes lies the heavenly Child,
More lovely than angels, this baby so mild.

Oh, there lies the Christ Child, on hay and on straw;
The shepherds are kneeling before him with awe.
And Mary and Joseph smile on him with love,
While angels are singing sweet songs from above.

—CHRISTOPH VON SCHMID, 1794

ADULT CHALLENGE

Make a list of spiritual goals. Include goals for a month, a year, five years, and ten years. Be as specific as possible in each category, then place this list before the Lord, pray about it, and determine to grow in your faith.

CHILD PROMPT

The age I look forward to most is _____ because _____

_____

_____

_____.

The age I feel was most special so far is ___ because _____

_____

_____.

ADVENT

Week

4

He Is Coming

Day 1

Choices and Consequences

READ

Jeremiah 33:1–16

KEY VERSES

"'In those days and at that time I will make a righteous Branch sprout from David's line; he will do what is just and right in the land. In those days Judah will be saved and Jerusalem will live in safety. This is the name by which it will be called: The LORD Our Righteousness.'" (Jer. 33:15–16)

My daughter very specifically told my granddaughter *not* to open the peanut butter but to put the jar away. The two-year-old, testing her will against her mother's, opened the jar anyway. Consequences followed.

As a grandparent I find myself occasionally shaking my head at the choices my adult children make with their kids. Sometimes I wonder what causes them to behave in one particular way or another. Since they are adults I only can give advice—and as every grandparent knows, unless they ask for it, it's usually unwelcome. Even though I care what happens in their lives, they need to make their own decisions and then deal with the consequences.

God must shake his head often when he deals with us, his children. Long before Jesus arrived, God had a plan for his chosen people, but still they made wrong choices. They turned their backs on God and chose to go in many other directions. He was angry, and they had to deal with the consequences.

But God made a promise. He would send a Savior who would take the burden of sin. This Savior came in the form of an infant babe in Bethlehem. He was not recognized as the Messiah by many of God's people. He was scorned, mocked, and finally put to death on a cross. Surely God must have shaken his head at the choices of his children. It must have hurt God that he would have to sacrifice someone so fine for something so wrong: his perfect Son for our sins. But God proved again that he is good and his love endures forever.

The first choice we should make is to accept this wonderful gift. Jesus came as a little baby, and he will come again so that we may live with him forever. Our next choice is to serve him and trust him in our lives as we wait for his return. As we wait expectantly and choose God, we will live abundantly and with joy and peace just as he promised.

CONSIDER

1. As you look back on your life, do you see where choices you made may have caused your parents to "shake their heads" with worry? If you had it to do all over again, would you make the same choices?
2. Do you feel you have made some choices that would cause our Lord to "shake his head"?

FAMILY ACTIVITY
Make Christmas wassail punch ✿

People in many countries around the world create a hot beverage that's to be shared in Christmas celebrations. Depending on the country, it may be a mulled cider, a spiced ale, or a sweetened milk drink. In England, this is called wassail punch. With great fanfare, festivities, and the singing of Christmas carols (especially the one about wassail itself), the hot punch is shared with family and friends.

The original Anglo-Saxon words *waes hael* mean "in good health" and over the centuries the words were used as a toast when drinking to someone's well-being, becoming the modern English word *wassail*. It was made years ago with wine, ale, or other spirits, apples, spices, sometimes eggs and cream, and other ingredients. The following recipe for Christmas wassail is not an exact replica of the original, but enjoy it in honor of the people who have celebrated the birth of Jesus in times past.

Christmas Wassail

1 gallon	apple cider
25–30	whole cloves
6–10	cinnamon sticks
1 quart	pineapple juice
1	6-ounce can frozen orange juice concentrate

Mix all ingredients in a large pot and simmer. Serve hot. (8–12 servings)

Joy to the World

Joy to the world! The Lord is come.
Let earth receive her King;
Let every heart
Prepare him room
And heaven and nature sing,
And heaven and nature sing,
And heaven, and heaven, and nature sing.

Joy to the world, the Savior reigns.
Let men their songs employ
While fields and floods
rocks, hills, and plains
Repeat the sounding joy,
Repeat the sounding joy,
Repeat, repeat, the sounding joy.

No more let sins and sorrows grow,
Nor thorns infest the ground;
He comes to make his blessings flow
Far as the curse is found,
Far as the curse is found,
Far as, far as the curse is found.

He rules the world with truth and grace
And makes the nations prove
The glories of his righteousness
And wonders of his love,
And wonders of his love,
And wonders, and wonders of his love

—Isaac Watts, 1719

ADULT CHALLENGE

Choices are part of our everyday life. Take a few minutes to list your priorities for the next year. Beside each priority, note briefly *why* it is important. Bring your list before the Lord and ask for his guidance.

CHILD PROMPT

One of the ways that I figure out what is most important is by _____
_____.

My mom or dad helps me make good decisions when they

_____

_____.

Day 2

Another Name for Love

READ
John 1:1-13

KEY VERSES
Yet to all who received him, to those who believed in his name, he gave the right to become children of God—children born not of natural descent, nor of human decision or a husband's will, but born of God. (Jn. 1:12-13)

Many years ago friends of ours adopted a beautiful Korean baby. Years later, they adopted another child with a huge array of physical disabilities. In addition to these children they have four biological children and have been host parents to countless other foster children. They have big hearts with enough love to share, so that no child within their reach would feel left out, neglected, or unloved. Every child became truly their own. Each was treated and cared for equally according to their needs, no matter what their social background, medical needs, or psychological issues. This required endless hours without sleep, as well as an enormous amount of patience and fortitude.

God has a heart big enough to encompass all his children, just like my friends. God's love surpasses all we can imagine. He wants us to accept his love and return this gift by simply serving him. God has the capacity to love each of us equally. God doesn't care about our nationality, race, gender, or financial situation. We have the opportunity to be adopted into the family of God by receiving and believing him.

We will one day join him and live with him forever if we make him the Lord of our lives. We will feel loved and accepted in his family. As we continue this Advent season, we might ask ourselves, "How can I become part of the family of God, and show my love for him, more completely?"

CONSIDER

1. It can be difficult to know how to love a God we cannot see or touch. How do you express your love for God?
2. How would you describe the difference between loving God and loving a member of your family?

FAMILY ACTIVITY
Create and give an invitation to your Christmas Eve service

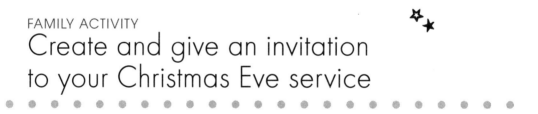

Christmas traditions can begin with a single family's idea. One family will share their idea with another family, and they with another family, and on and on until an entire region may share what has become a tradition. The following idea can be shared over and over again in the hopes that more and more families attend the Christmas Eve service to celebrate the birth of the Christ Child. Each family member can make an invitation to share—they need not be identical, but personal, designed for the person receiving it.

MATERIALS NEEDED

- construction paper or colored art paper
- stickers
- pencils
- markers, pens, or crayons
- information on your church's Christmas Eve service

Fold a piece of construction paper or colored art paper into quarters. On the outside front write "A Special Invitation for You" at the top (or another introduction of your choice). Apply Christmas stickers throughout the center of the card for decoration, or make an appropriate drawing. On the bottom of the front write "Rejoice with Us on Christmas Eve" (or another statement of your choice).

Also decorate the inside left-hand side of the card. On the inside right, at the top write "Please Join Us in Celebration!" Then write "Time" below and add the time the service will begin. Below "time," write "Date" and add "December 24," and finally write "Place" beneath the date and fill in where the Christmas Eve service will be held. Give the invitation to someone you would like to invite to your Christmas Eve service.

The First Noel

The first Noel the angels did say
Was to certain poor shepherds in fields as
    they lay,
In fields where they lay keeping their sheep
On a cold winter's night that was so deep.

Refrain:
Noel, Noel, Noel, Noel!
Born is the King of Israel!

They looked up and saw a star
Shining in the East beyond them far,
And to the earth it gave great light,
And so it continued both day and night.
[Refrain]

And by the light of that same star
Three Wise Men came from country far,
To seek for a King was their intent
And to follow the star wherever it went.
[Refrain]

This star drew nigh to the northwest
O'er Bethlehem it took its rest,
And there it did both pause and stay
Right o'er the place where Jesus lay.
[Refrain]

Then entered in those Wise Men three
Full reverently upon their knee,
And offered there in his presence
Their gold and myrrh and frankincense.
[Refrain]

Then let us all with one accord
Sing praises to our heavenly Lord
That hath made heaven and earth of
    nought
And with his blood mankind has bought.
[Refrain]

—ENGLISH CAROL, seventeenth century

ADULT CHALLENGE

Consider "adopting" a person or a family who is in some way different from your own, perhaps a family from your church that is going through difficult times this Christmas season. Create a plan for the next several weeks (or whatever time frame suits you) during which you supply them on a regular basis with a card, a phone call, a home-cooked dinner, fruit, small necessities, a gift card, or any other gift that displays caring as Jesus would. Be as creative as you like! You may choose to do this anonymously, or you may want to inquire ahead of time if he/she/they would like to be "adopted" by you. Realize that reaching out in this way will help you as much or more as it helps the other person!

CHILD PROMPT

I know that I am loved when_____

_____

_____.

Day 3

Good Work!

READ
Philippians 1:1–11

KEY VERSES
In all my prayers for all of you, I always pray with joy because of your partnership in the gospel from the first day until now, being confident of this, that he who began a good work in you will carry it on to completion until the day of Christ Jesus. (Phil. 1:4–6)

I have many interests I would like to pursue: playing a musical instrument, watercolor painting, calligraphy, studying weather phenomena, researching family genealogy, making cards to mail, and on and on! I know, however, that if I started a project in any of these areas, the chances of my continuing over a long period of time would be slim. Other priorities always seem to take their place.

But unlike all these passing interests, I have discovered I really love to quilt. I find this activity soothing and calming even after a hard day's work. I've heard quilting can actually lower your blood pressure. But still I don't always have the time I'd like to spend doing it. Since it's common for me to have four or five projects going at the same time, some of my quilts have taken as long as ten years or more to finish.

In today's verse, Paul was writing to the early church at Philippi. He was joyful because they kept the faith. They believed in Jesus and knew the value of sharing God's gospel. They were living their lives according to the model set before them. The Philippians were certain that even if they didn't see their reward here on earth, they would one day receive the greatest prize of all—joining Jesus in the hereafter in heaven. This promise kept them motivated!

This is just as true today as it was then. God has given each of us an important mission to complete—important enough that we need to give it our best effort each day. Unlike my quilting, which I can lay aside when life gets too busy, God's work must never be tabled.

CONSIDER

1. Do you have one particular activity or project you enjoy? Have you created a timetable for completion, or is time not an issue?
2. Is there work that you do for the kingdom of God? What is it?

FAMILY ACTIVITY
Discuss the role and importance of the participants in the Christmas story

As we continue to move toward Christmas and ask ourselves, "Why are we waiting?" it is a good time to reflect on the participants of the first Christmas. They include the angel who visited Mary, the angel who visited Zechariah, Mary, her cousin Elizabeth, Joseph, Herod, the innkeeper, the shepherds, and the Wise Men.

MATERIALS NEEDED

- a Bible
- a concordance

Look up the Scripture verses about each of the participants mentioned above. Read and then discuss the "work" they did in the story. Open the discussion about their "work" and see where it takes you. Additional questions may include these: How do you think they felt? How would you have reacted given the same situation? What would it take in today's world to make the same events happen? How would the events unfold?

When the discussion is finished, reread the Christmas story in Luke chapter 2. End in prayer.

Angels We Have Heard on High

Angels we have heard on high
Sweetly singing o'er the plains
And the mountains in reply,
Echoing their joyous strains.

Refrain:
Gloria
in excelsis Deo
Gloria
in excelsis Deo

Shepherds, why this jubilee?
Why your joyous strains prolong?
What the gladsome tidings be
Which inspire your heavenly song?
[*Refrain*]

Come to Bethlehem and see
Him whose birth the angels sing;
Come, adore on bended knee
Christ, the Lord, the newborn King
[*Refrain*]

See him in a manger laid
Jesus, Lord of heaven and earth!
Mary, Joseph, lend your aid,
With us sing our Savior's birth.
[*Refrain*]

—FRENCH CAROL, translated by James
Chadwick in 1862

ADULT CHALLENGE

Are you involved in any kind of activity in your church? Is there a specific "project" before you? If not, consider a way to create one. Be as creative as you can.

CHILD PROMPT

Some things I would like to do before I become an adult are _____

_____

_____.

Some things I would like to do as an adult include _____

_____.

Day 4

Journey toward Connection

READ

Luke 2:4–5

KEY VERSE

So Joseph also went up from the town of Nazareth in Galilee to Judea, to Bethlehem the town of David, because he belonged to the house and line of David. (Lk. 2:4)

A friend of mine recently traveled to New York City. Along with sightseeing, part of the reason for the trip was to track down records of when her grandparents arrived on Ellis Island. Her searching led her to conclude they must have arrived in America in 1895.

It isn't a requirement to know your lineage, but we are required to register when there's a census, as Joseph was required to do when he left Nazareth for Bethlehem because he "belonged to the house and line of David." For my friend, and many others like her, there is a need within to journey back in their history to find connections with their past. This helps fill a void about who they are, where they came from, and what their family represents.

As part of the family of God, there are those today who make the journey to the Holy Land in Galilee where Jesus was born. This somehow completes their connection with their past. It's important to their identity as Christians to see the places where Jesus walked and taught.

On an even more basic (and accessible) level, we should all take time to journey back spiritually to find where our faith began, to focus on what is important, and to remind ourselves of God's love.

CONSIDER

1. Have you ever taken a "spiritual journey" back to your roots to consider how you came to know God?
2. If you look back over your family history, where in your family line did Christian faith first originate?

FAMILY ACTIVITY
Experience the journey of Mary and Joseph to Bethlehem

Read the Christmas story as a family this year (perhaps even have the child closest to the age of ten do the reading) and consider the trip Mary and Joseph made to Bethlehem. The following activity will aid you on their journey.

MATERIALS NEEDED

- Scripture from Luke chapter 2
- a map of Israel
- reference material such as can be obtained from an Internet connection or a library

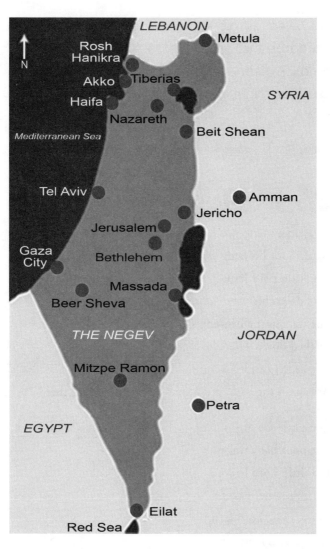

Do a search on the Internet (type in "journey of Mary and Joseph" without quotation marks in your search engine) to find the route Mary and Joseph might have taken to Bethlehem. Determine the time it might have taken and the distance they traveled. Consider what they might have eaten and where they may have taken rest along the way. Determine also what hazards they might have faced on their journey. Mark the route on the map. Then compare the information gleaned on the route, the time frame, the distance, and the hazards a person might encounter if they took the same journey today.

• •

Away in a Manger

Away in a manger,
No crib for his bed,
The little Lord Jesus
Laid down his sweet head;
The stars in the heavens
Looked down where he lay,
The little Lord Jesus
Asleep on the hay.

The cattle are lowing,
The poor baby wakes,
But little Lord Jesus,
No crying he makes.
I love Thee, Lord Jesus;
Look down from the sky
And stay by my cradle
Till morning is nigh.

Be near me, Lord Jesus;
I ask thee to stay
Close by me forever
And love me, I pray!
Bless all the dear children
In thy tender care,
And fit us for heaven
To live with thee there.

—WILLIAM J. KIRKPATRICK, 1895

ADULT CHALLENGE

Create a family tree that includes your parents, grandparents, brothers, sisters, aunts, uncles, nieces, nephews, and grandchildren. Find out, if you can, which of these people have (or had) a strong faith. Pray for them all.

CHILD PROMPT

The adult I admire the most is _____

because _____

_____.

Day 5

Good News!

READ
Luke 2:1-20

KEY VERSES
But the angel said to them, "Do not be afraid. I bring you good news of great joy that will be for all the people. Today in the town of David a Savior has been born to you; he is Christ the Lord." (Lk. 2:10-11)

Friends of mine hoped for many years to have a child and were disappointed countless times. The waiting was painful and arduous. Finally, their prayers were answered and the couple's anguished waiting turned to excitement and joy with the healthy arrival of their first child.

For my husband and me, the birth of a child is an extraordinary event. And with every new grandchild who comes along, we are as excited as we were when our first child was born.

Imagine waiting hundreds of years for the Messiah. God's people were promised a Savior, and he finally arrived as a newborn. The waiting ended at last. He didn't come in stately manner and with high honor. Instead he came as a poor infant in deplorable conditions, in a manger in an animal stable. Yet the angels declared to the shepherds there was reason for celebration, joy, and praising!

Then came time for action. The shepherds decided to find this special child. Their journey, led by a bright star, brought them to Jesus. They knew their lives would never be the same, even though they had no idea how the prophecies would all be fulfilled. Their expectation of a Savior had given rise to joy and a completeness that otherwise they could not have attained.

We have the opportunity to experience the same expectation and excitement the shepherds felt so long ago. That little baby has the potential to fill us with a completeness that only he can give. It is with this joy that we come to Christmas. We are filled with great expectation about what our Savior will do for the world for which he came, and we are filled with honor to be able to come to him, as the shepherds did, and give him our best. It won't be gold, frankincense, or myrrh as the Wise Men gave, but we can give him our heart, our souls, our very lives!

CONSIDER

1. Reflect on all the gifts you have purchased for Christmas. Do they reflect your heart and soul or the way you want to live your life? Is there something you might give to a loved one, in addition, that speaks more clearly of these things?

2. Do you find it difficult to wait for something you have longed for? Would you have been more of an innkeeper, a shepherd, or a wise man?

"Good News!" Puzzle

The Christmas celebration is like none other. There is joy for all people who embrace the Christ Child.

Use the numbers along the path to find the words in Luke 2, the verses that announce this grand celebration. Write the letter from the path that corresponds to the number on the blank line. For example, the number 6 = the letter *q*; 25 = the letter *p*.

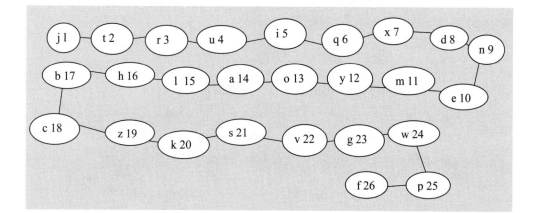

17 4 2   2 16 10   14 9 23 10 15   21 14 5 8   2 13   2 16 10 11   "8 13   9 13 2

_____   _____   _____   _____   _____   _____   _____   _____

17 10   14 26 3 14 5 8   5   17 3 5 9 23   12 13 4   23 13 13 8   9 10 24 21

_____   _____   _____   _____   _____   _____   _____

13 26   23 3 10 14 2   1 13 12   2 16 14 2   24 5 15 15   17 10   26 13 3

_____   _____   _____   _____   _____   _____   _____

14 15 15   2 16 10   25 10 13 25 15 10   2 13 8 14 12   5 9   2 16 10

_____   _____   _____   _____   _____   _____

2 13 24 9   13 26   8 14 22 5 8   14   21 14 22 5 13 3   16 14 21

_____   _____   _____   _____   _____   _____

17 10 10 9   17 13 3 9   2 13   12 13 4   16 10   5 21   18 16 3 5 21 2

_____   _____   _____   _____   _____   _____   _____

2 16 10   15 13 3 8"

_____   _____   (from Luke 2)   Find the answer on page 151.

Love Came Down at Christmas

Love came down at Christmas,
Love all lovely, love divine;
Love was born at Christmas,
Star and angels gave the sign.

Worship we the Godhead,
Love incarnate, love divine;
Worship we our Jesus:
But wherewith for sacred sign?

Love shall be our token,
Love shall be yours and love be mine,
Love to God and to all men,
Love for plea and gift and sign.

—CHRISTINA ROSSETTI, 1885

ADULT CHALLENGE

Consider what gift of yourself you can give to God. Make it as personal as possible. Write your gift on a piece of paper, seal it in an envelope, and place it under your tree or somewhere nearby so it is clearly part of your gifts to be given. When you open your other gifts, open your envelope to God. Offer a prayer for your gift and resolve to follow through with your plan.

CHILD PROMPT

The greatest gift I can give to Jesus during this next year is _____

_____

_____ .

Day 6

From a Long Line

READ

Matthew 1:1–17

KEY VERSE

And Jacob the father of Joseph, the husband of Mary, of whom was born Jesus, who is called Christ. (Matt. 1:16)

Jesus is the Christ. He was born during the rule of Augustus Caesar, in Judea in the town of Bethlehem. He came from the line of David, as prophesied centuries before. There were fourteen generations from Abraham to David, fourteen generations from David to the exile to Babylon, and fourteen generations from the exile to the birth of Jesus. The Bible cites each of these in Matthew chapter 1.

Jesus knew who he was. He didn't question his lineage as the Son of God. He knew his purpose. It was to become the perfect Lamb for a lost world. His lineage and purpose have become linked with our own. We can know who we truly are when we live as children of God. God in Christ makes us who we are. We are by nature human, sinners, much less than perfect. Yet because Jesus gave his life we can be part of the family of God.

This is the most perfect gift we can have or receive this Christmas season!

CONSIDER

1. Do you know who you are?

2. Does the life you lead in the here-and-now make clear to others what you believe and stand for?

FAMILY ACTIVITY
Make luminaries

Luminaries are an inexpensive and beautiful way to light an area with cheerfulness. Luminaries are often used along walkways or driveways for decorative lighting. Many believe that they began as a Spanish tradition of lighting the way for the Christ Child during Advent. You can create your own to welcome and light the way for your guests to your home out of the dark (and perhaps cold) in these final days before Christmas Day.

MATERIALS NEEDED

- lunch bags in your color preference: regular brown ones are just fine, but red and green ones are available
- or you can reuse plastic gallon milk jugs with the tops neatly cut off
- long-burning votive candles
- sand or kitty litter for weighting the bags
- markers
- stencils
- hole punch

If using bags, fold down the tops about an inch and then fold down again. This will help stabilize the bags. (For further stabilization you may choose to cut a cardboard square the size of the bag bottom. Place the cut cardboard into the bottom of the bag before going any further.) If using milk jugs, continue with the directions as you would the bags.

Pour two inches of sand or three inches of kitty litter in the bottom of each bag or jug. Place the bags or jugs one to two feet apart along the area planned for lighting. Carefully burrow the candle into the sand or litter so it won't fall over. At dusk, using a long lighter (like those used on a grill) light the candles. Enjoy!

Make sure all candles are out before retiring for the night. If you wait until morning to take up the bags, remember the bottoms may be wet, so lift with care in case the bottoms begin to fall out.

ADULT CHALLENGE
Consider your convictions regarding your faith, your family, your career, and your goals. Write down a few of these. Are you surprised with what you've written?

CHILD PROMPT
The values I learn from my parents can best be seen in me when _____

_____

_____.

Day 7

Unwrapping the Gift

READ

Isaiah 9:2–7

KEY VERSE

For to us a child is born, to us a son is given, and the government will be on his shoulders. And he will be called Wonderful Counselor, Mighty God, Everlasting Father, Prince of Peace. (Isa. 9:6)

Children are a delight to watch as they open their Christmas gifts. Their eyes are glowing, their bodies jumping with enthusiasm, barely able to contain their glee. With a great rush they tear off the paper to reveal their prizes.

While there are some adults who also open gifts in a rush like a child, there are those like my mother-in-law who savor every single minute. She was careful not to tear the paper, slowly tugging at the tape, trying not even to leave a scar where the tape had been.

The greatest gift, however, was opened for us long ago. It was the gift of Jesus. He was promised years before he arrived.

This precious gift would be called the "Wonderful Counselor" who encompasses all understanding. Not only does Jesus understand the questions in our hearts and minds, but he also understands how we feel, and he understands the answers. He knows what is best for us.

He's also called "Mighty God." This means that there's no problem too big for God to handle. He has the power not only to implement his will but also to accomplish his will in our lives. We can bring our problems to God no matter how large or small they are. His power is beyond what our human minds can imagine.

Third, he is called "Everlasting Father." A father's love can be profound; I know my father's was. Jesus labors to meet the needs of his children. He loves them despite how they may disappoint him. His desire is to provide for them until they are able to care for themselves. But of course, our human fathers grow old and pass on—this often leaves us grieving for their companionship and advice. Jesus promises that he will never leave. We need only breathe his name to commune with Jesus at any time of day. He's always there!

Last, he is called "Prince of Peace." Peace is something many people fail to have and earnestly long for. Their lives are filled with sadness, pain, desolation, fear, and anxiety. Jesus promises peace, a peace that passes all understanding. This Christmas, unwrap the greatest gift of all. We can open ourselves to Christ with the excitement of a child and draw him close to our hearts with joy and delight. Or we can open ourselves to him slowly, savoring every single gift that he brings.

CONSIDER

1. How do you show your excitement when a gift is just what you wanted? Remember a Christmas gift that was most meaningful to you.
2. Which of the four gifts mentioned in our Scripture for today do you feel that you need most of all right now?

FAMILY ACTIVITY
Name search

MATERIALS NEEDED

- ■ a Bible
- ■ a baby name book, or Internet or library research resources

Jesus was promised in Isaiah 7:14 many years before the event of his birth occurred. In Matthew 1:23 an angel spoke to Joseph, explaining that his betrothed, Mary, would bear a son and his name would be Jesus, and that he would be called "Immanuel," which means "God with us."

There are many different names throughout the Bible that refer to God, and they help us understand who he is.

Do a search online (type in your search engine "names of God") to look up the different names of God and what each means. Make a chart of your findings. It might look something like this:

Name	Scripture	Meaning	What It Tells of God's Character

Then make a list of the names in your family, including extended family if desired. Use a baby name book or the Internet to find what each name means. (Type "baby names" in your search engine if you are doing a search online.) Create another chart to apply your findings and determine if the names seem to fit the person to which they belong. It might look something like this:

Name	Meaning	Applies (yes or no)

Ask your family members if they like the name given to them. If they could choose their own names, ask what they would choose and have each person tell why.

ADULT CHALLENGE

In what area of your life do you need understanding? Write it on a slip of paper. Do you have a problem that feels overwhelming? Write it on another slip of paper. Last, do you need peace about something in your life? Write it on another slip of paper. Place each of these an envelope. Seal it. Write the date on the outside. Give the issues to God. Perhaps talk with a trusted friend about them. Ask the friend to pray for you. At a later time (a month, three months, or longer), open your envelope and see what God has done for you.

CHILD PROMPT

I open gifts with eagerness and enthusiasm because _____
_____
_____. Opening gifts slowly would be hard
because _____
_____.

Christmastide
He Has Come

Christmas Eve

A Special Relationship

READ

Romans 5:1–11

KEY VERSE

Not only is this so, but we also rejoice in God through our Lord Jesus Christ, through whom we have now received reconciliation. (Rom. 5:11)

I have three daughters and two sons. I am close to my daughters, but I was concerned the same would not be true when I began having daughters-in-law. After all, they would have their own mothers with whom they can relate and who know them well. But I am pleased to say that I have a great relationship with my first daughter-in-law. This wonderful young woman is everything I would want in a daughter. She's kind, witty, attractive, warm, and gentle. I rejoice in our relationship. I envision days of discussions, shopping, walking, and a myriad of ways that will deepen our friendship over the years to come.

By having a relationship with God, we have the open invitation to chat with him about anything, whether it's something serious or it's sharing good news. He honestly is interested in what we have to say! This relationship isn't one-sided, where we do all the talking and God does all the listening. It's most effective when we slow down, open our hearts and our minds, and let God talk with us. It is in these times when we will find God's will for our lives, comfort when things are bad, joy in simple things or even troubles, and unconditional love that alters how we experience the world.

On this Christmas Eve, there are many people who are searching for something to fill a void in their lives. People are looking for the kind of love and peace that only Christ can give. They are searching for understanding, comfort, and companionship that cannot be filled through human means.

Jesus Christ came to this earth so that all of our souls would be filled. It is only through him that our lives are complete. Until our souls find the perfect love that can only come from Jesus, we will search endlessly. Christmas Eve is ultimately about the best relationship of all.

CONSIDER

1. What qualities do you consider important to being a friend?

2. Whom do you consider your closest friend? What makes that person so?

FAMILY ACTIVITY

Make Christmas Eve special for someone who is alone

MATERIALS NEEDED

- a book
- a magazine
- cookies, a box of candy, cake bread, or another baked item
- or another gift that might be special to someone who is alone this Christmas

Christmas Eve is the traditional night for many family gatherings and attending a worship service. There are people who have no family near, and there are elderly persons who would enjoy attending the service but have no means to get there. Deliver a gift for a neighbor or an acquaintance who is alone this Christmas, or offer a ride for someone who otherwise would be unable to attend the service.

Once in Royal David's City

Once in royal David's city,
Stood a lowly cattle shed,
Where a mother laid her baby
In a manger for his bed:
Mary was that mother mild,
Jesus Christ her little child.

He came down to earth from heaven,
Who is God and Lord of all,
And his shelter was a stable,
And his cradle was a stall;
With the poor and meek and lowly,
Lived on earth our Savior holy.

And, through all his wondrous childhood,
He would honor and obey,
Love and watch the lowly maiden,
In whose gentle arms he lay.
Christian children all should be,
Mild, obedient, good as he.

And our eyes at last shall see him,
Through his own redeeming love;
For that Child who seemed so helpless,
Is our Lord in heaven above,
And he leads his children on,
To the place where he is gone.

Not in that poor lowly stable,
With the oxen standing by,
We shall see him, but in heaven,
Set at God's right hand on high;
When like stars his children crowned,
All in white shall be around.

—CECIL FRANCES ALEXANDER, 1848

ADULT CHALLENGE

Make a list of three acquaintances. Follow that list with three friends. Make a third list of your three closest friends. Determine what makes each list different. Are you more of an acquaintance, a friend, or a close friend of God?

CHILD PROMPT

My most favorite person who is not in my family is _____

because _____.

I will _____

to make our friendship even stronger.

Christmas Day

New Kid in Town

READ
1 John 5:1–11

KEY VERSE
And this is the testimony: God has given us eternal life, and this life is in his Son. (1 Jn. 5:11)

I recently heard the Christmas song "There's a New Kid in Town," a popular holiday recording for several country stars including Kathy Mattea and George Strait. The song tells the story of someone searching for the Messiah in Bethlehem. The response of the person answering was that he heard there was a "new kid in town." This, of course, was the baby Jesus. This child ultimately became the hope of those who came to find him.

It is true that Jesus was the new kid in town. But also, imagine how the shepherds must have felt as they left their fields in search of a Savior. The shepherds were excited and accepted the challenge of finding the baby as described by the angels, because they believed God had spoken to them through those angels who brought good tidings of great joy. The Wise Men followed a star. God said it, so they believed it. It was as simple as that.

Wouldn't it be wonderful if we took God's word at face value and believed it just because God said it, as the shepherds and Wise Men did? His word promises eternal life and a relationship with this Christ Child it will change every other aspect of our lives. Christmas isn't just something that happened long ago in a faraway place—it isn't just a good story; it can happen in us.

Don't miss the "new kid"—the child, Jesus. And I hope that you can approach him this year as a new kid yourself. There is no source of comfort and joy in what the world offers that's comparable to what a relationship with Jesus will bring.

CONSIDER

1. Have you ever been the "new kid in town"? How did that make you feel?

2. How are you approaching the child Jesus this year in a way that may be different from that of other years?

FAMILY ACTIVITY
Celebrate the birth of a child born on Christmas Day

We celebrate Christmas Day as the birthday of Jesus. Other children throughout the world are also born on this date every year. They share a special birthday with the Messiah. Celebrate the birth of a newborn who shares this day with the Christ. Give a gift to commemorate the day, even if it's a newborn you do not know, just as the Wise Men and shepherds, upon their visit to Jesus, had not before been introduced!

MATERIALS NEEDED

- a new or almost new ornament
- craft glue
- tempera paint
- a marker or other means to decorate an ornament
- or purchase an ornament already decorated
- paper/pen/etc., and envelope to write a note to accompany your gift

Obtain an ornament by purchasing an already decorated one, creating one, or removing one from your tree that can be used as a special gift to a newborn. Decorate the ornament. You may choose to paint or use a marker to carefully write "Baby's First Christmas" if desired, or just write the date or write "special baby," "Christmas baby," or something else you desire if there is adequate space to do so. You also may want to decorate the ornament by attaching ribbon with craft glue, or decorate it in another way that makes it feel special.

Write a note telling the recipient of your motives behind the gift. Indicate that they share a special day with the birth of Jesus and you wish to add to their joy. Have family members sign their names if possible. (You may only want to write first names.)

As a family, visit a nearby hospital. Inquire at the information desk before going further to obtain permission or to learn of the proper channels to give your gift. It may be necessary to leave it to be delivered by a nurse from the maternity ward floor to the unsuspecting family. As you leave, pray together for the health and happiness of that child.

With Wondering Awe

With wondering awe the Wise Men saw
The star in heaven springing,
And with delight, in peaceful night,
They heard the angel singing.

Refrain:
Hosanna, hosanna! Hosanna to his name!

By light of star they traveled far
To seek the lowly manger,
A humble bed wherein was laid
The wondrous little Stranger.
[Refrain]

And still is found, the world around,
The old and hallowed story,
And still is sung in every tongue
The angels' song of glory:
[Refrain]

The heavenly star its rays afar
On every land is throwing,
And shall not cease till holy peace
In all the earth is growing.
[Refrain]

—Anonymous, published in *Laudis Corona*, 1885

ADULT CHALLENGE

Consider the newborns and their families in your community, at work, or church. Could one or more of the families use your help in some way?

CHILD PROMPT

When I see a new baby I usually think _____

_____ .

To make the new baby special to me, I could _____

_____ .

Onward

Sowing Seeds

READ

Luke 8:4–15

KEY VERSE

But the seed on good soil stands for those with a noble and good heart, who hear the word, retain it, and by persevering produce a crop.
(Luke 8:15)

My two-and-a-half-year-old granddaughter absolutely loves her granddaddy! When he is on the tractor, she asks repeatedly, "I ride?" While in the garden, she is right beside him reaching for his hand. When he is working on automobiles, she's there—even though she hasn't a clue what he's doing. When he crosses his arms, she crosses hers. When his hands are in his pockets, hers are too. When he runs his fingers through his hair, she reaches up to adjust hers. It is with great determination and much observation that she follows his example as close to the letter as she can. This man has much influence on this tiny child.

Our Scripture talks about planting seeds. In Luke 8 we find seeds sown along the path and hearts that hear but cannot believe. Seeds are sown on rock and heard with joy, but the seeds die when tested by the things of this world, because there is no root. Seeds that fall among thorns demonstrate the word is heard, but life's worries, riches, and pleasures keep the seeds from maturing and being productive. Finally, seed falls on rich, fertile ground; the word is heard, accepted, and retained, and it becomes the source of a good crop.

We have the responsibility to be in relationships that are like seeds planted in rich soil. My husband has a great responsibility to our little granddaughter. What he tells her she will accept readily and no doubt greedily because of their relationship. This also requires that he be careful in what he says and how he reacts to different situations around her because of his influence.

This bond is much like what we share with our Savior. We can learn much if we open our hearts, minds, and spirits to his word and allow it to influence our lives. That influence, in turn, will be projected to those around us, providing the perfect atmosphere for sowing seeds in rich soil. It also requires us to be as close to what Jesus wants us to be as possible. In this way we are planting seeds that will fall on good, fertile soil!

CONSIDER

1. With whom do you have the closest relationships? What makes each of those relationships as close as they are?
2. Do you spend time with God in the same ways that you spend time with the people who are closest to you?

FAMILY ACTIVITY
Plant a seed

• •

Christians in Lebanon begin their celebration of Christmas in a unique way. About two weeks before the Christmas holiday they plant a variety of different seeds in cotton wool or soil, making sure to water them daily. The idea is to plant the seeds so they will grow about six inches tall by Christmas. The plants are then used to decorate the Nativity scenes on Christmas morning. Family and friends exchange foods and good wishes and then share lunch as the generations join together to eat the most important meal, on the most important holiday of the year.

You can do this, too—even if you live in an apartment building or in the cold, white north!

MATERIALS NEEDED

- a small flowerpot for each member of the family (a plastic cup will also work)
- potting soil
- water
- seeds

Fill each small flowerpot with potting soil about three-quarters full. Add several seeds to the soil and water moderately. Place in a warm, sunny window to watch the plant grow. For the plant to thrive, you have the responsibility to make sure the soil doesn't dry out completely and the plant gets plenty of sun, preferably in the morning. You should see small sprouts in about a week.

If you do not have any flower seeds to plant, take five or six seeds from a cut tomato and place them on a napkin to dry overnight. Scrape the seeds off the napkin into the soil the next morning. Follow the same instructions as above.

Angels from the Realms of Glory

Angels from the realms of glory,
Wing your flight o'er all the earth;
Ye who sang creations story,
Now proclaim Messiah's birth:

Refrain:
Come and worship, come and worship,
Worship Christ the newborn King!

Shepherds in the fields abiding,
Watching over your flocks by night;
God with man is now residing,
Yonder shines the Infant light;
[Refrain]

Sages, leave your contemplations,
Brighter visions beam afar;
Seek the great desire of nations,
Ye have seen his natal star;
[Refrain]

Saints before the altar bending,
Watching long in hope and fear;
Suddenly the Lord, descending,
In his temple shall appear:
[Refrain]

—JAMES MONTGOMERY, 1816

ADULT CHALLENGE

Consider how you plant seeds with your life. You do this consciously as well as unconsciously in what you do and say and in how you are in the world. What sort of sowing have you done in the last year? Get in touch with one of your closest friends and discuss this issue. Ask the friend for some wisdom. God says that where two or three are gathered together in his name, he is present, too. Ask your friend, "Help me to see what God might want for my life in the coming year. What should I do to sow and reap better than I have this past year?"

CHILD PROMPT

I like growing things because _____.

As I grow taller and bigger I also want to grow in other ways, such as _____

_____.

Answers to Puzzles

"Service of the Heart" Puzzle

"I am the Lord's servant," Mary answered. "May it be to me as you have said." Then the angel left her. (Lk. 1:38)

Star Code Puzzle

"I, Jesus, have sent my angel to give you this testimony for the churches. I am the Root and the Offspring of David, and the bright Morning Star." (Rev. 22:16)

"Good News!" Puzzle

But the angel said to them, "Do not be afraid. I bring you good news of great joy that will be for all the people. Today in the town of David a Savior has been born to you; he is Christ the Lord." (Lk. 2:10–11)

Acknowledgments

I must first thank my Lord and Savior for giving me the opportunity to put on paper these thoughts and activities. I offer special thanks to Jon Sweeney for his help and belief in this project. Thanks also to my children and grandchildren, who have inadvertently given me a wealth of material over the years! And it is with heartfelt gratitude that I thank my wonderful husband, Charles, for all he gives and whose love and support I cherish.

Index

About Paraclete Press

Who We Are

Paraclete Press is a publisher of books, recordings, and DVDs on Christian spirituality. Our publishing represents a full expression of Christian belief and practice—from Catholic to Evangelical, from Protestant to Orthodox.

We are the publishing arm of the Community of Jesus, an ecumenical monastic community in the Benedictine tradition. As such, we are uniquely positioned in the marketplace without connection to a large corporation and with informal relationships to many branches and denominations of faith.

What We Are Doing

Books

Paraclete publishes books that show the richness and depth of what it means to be Christian. Although Benedictine spirituality is at the heart of all that we do, we publish books that reflect the Christian experience across many cultures, time periods, and houses of worship. We publish books that nourish the vibrant life of the church and its people—books about spiritual practice, formation, history, ideas, and customs.

We have several different series, including the best-selling Living Library, Paraclete Essentials, and Paraclete Giants series of classic texts in contemporary English; A Voice from the Monastery—men and women monastics writing about living a spiritual life today; award-winning literary faith fiction and poetry; and the Active Prayer Series that brings creativity and liveliness to any life of prayer.

Recordings

From Gregorian chant to contemporary American choral works, our music recordings celebrate sacred choral music through the centuries. Paraclete distributes the recordings of the internationally acclaimed choir Gloriæ Dei Cantores, praised for their "rapt and fathomless spiritual intensity" by *American Record Guide*, and the Gloriæ Dei Cantores Schola, which specializes in the study and performance of Gregorian chant. Paraclete is also the exclusive North American distributor of the recordings of the Monastic Choir of St. Peter's Abbey in Solesmes, France, long considered to be a leading authority on Gregorian chant.

DVDs

Our DVDs offer spiritual help, healing, and biblical guidance for life issues: grief and loss, marriage, forgiveness, anger management, facing death, and spiritual formation.

Learn more about us at our website: www.paracletepress.com
or call us toll-free at 1-800-451-5006.

You may also be interested in . . .

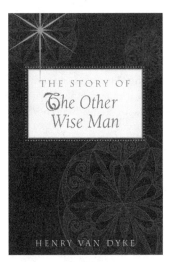

The Story of the Other Wise Man
by Henry van Dyke

One of the most meaningful stories ever written . . .

"You know the story of the Three Wise Men of the East, and how they traveled from far away to offer their gifts at the manger-cradle in Bethlehem. But have you ever heard the story of the Other Wise Man?"

So begins Henry van Dyke's Christmas classic, told in the manner of the great fairy tales—and like a great fairy tale, it couldn't be more true! This beautiful edition is designed so that you can read *The Other Wise Man* as it is intended to be read—slowly.

$14.95   Hardcover • ISBN: 978-1-55725-610-2

O Christmas Three
by O. Henry, Tolstoy, and Dickens

This beautiful gift book contains three heart-warming stories that recall Christmases past:

O. HENRY'S all-American tale "The Gift of the Magi," originally published in 1906.

LEO TOLSTOY'S Russian folktale "Where Love Is, There God Is Also" from 1887.

CHARLES DICKENS's little-known classic "What Christmas Is, As We Grow Older" from 1851.

$16.99   Hardcover • ISBN: 978-1-55725-776-5

Available from most booksellers or through Paraclete Press

www.paracletepress.com • 1-800-451-5006 • Try your local bookstore